CREEPY
KAWAii

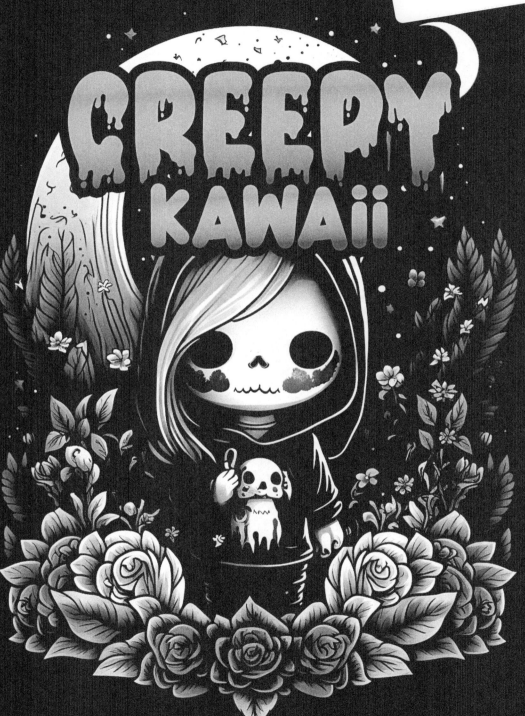

Dear Colorist Enthusiast,

I wanted to extend a heartfelt thank you for purchasing my coloring book. I hope the pages within will provide you with a sense of relaxation, peace, and creativity.

Amazon prints this book on a paper that is best suited for use with colored pencils and water-based markers. However, if you choose to use wet mediums, such as gel pens, make sure to place a sheet of paper underneath the page to avoid any ink bleed-through.

I aim to create products that bring joy and inspiration to my customers. If there is anything I can do to improve your experience with this coloring book, please do not hesitate to reach out to me. Your feedback is important to me and helps me continue to grow and improve.

I would be honored if you could take a moment to leave a review on Amazon after you have had a chance to enjoy this coloring book. Your support and feedback mean the world to me and will help me continue to create high-quality products.

Sincerely,

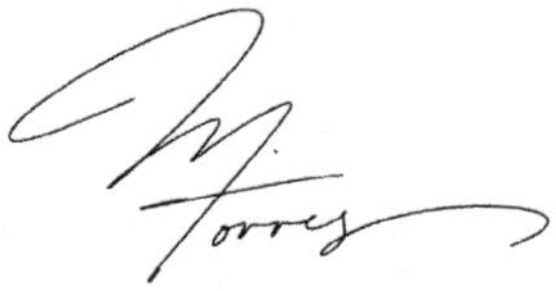

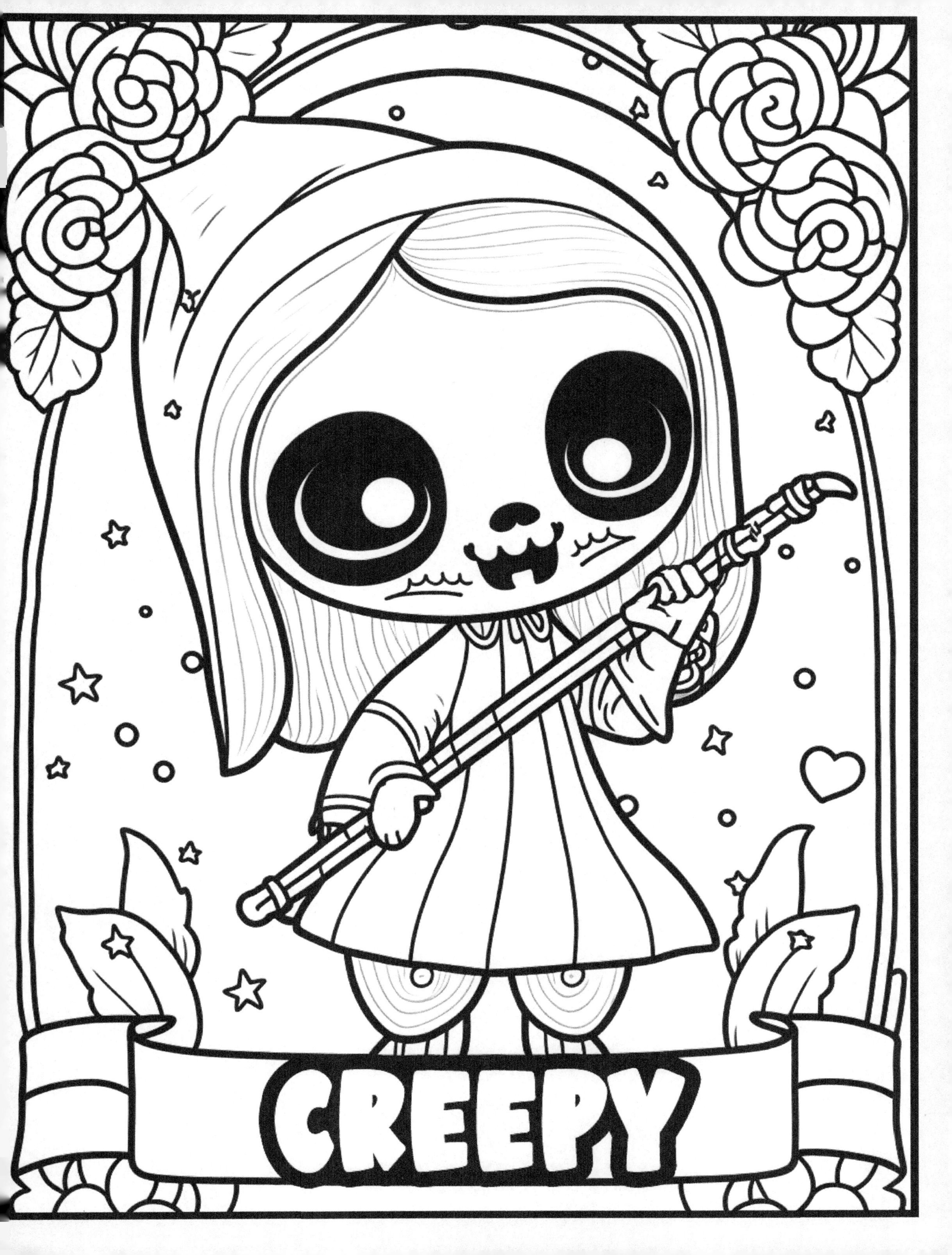
CREEPY

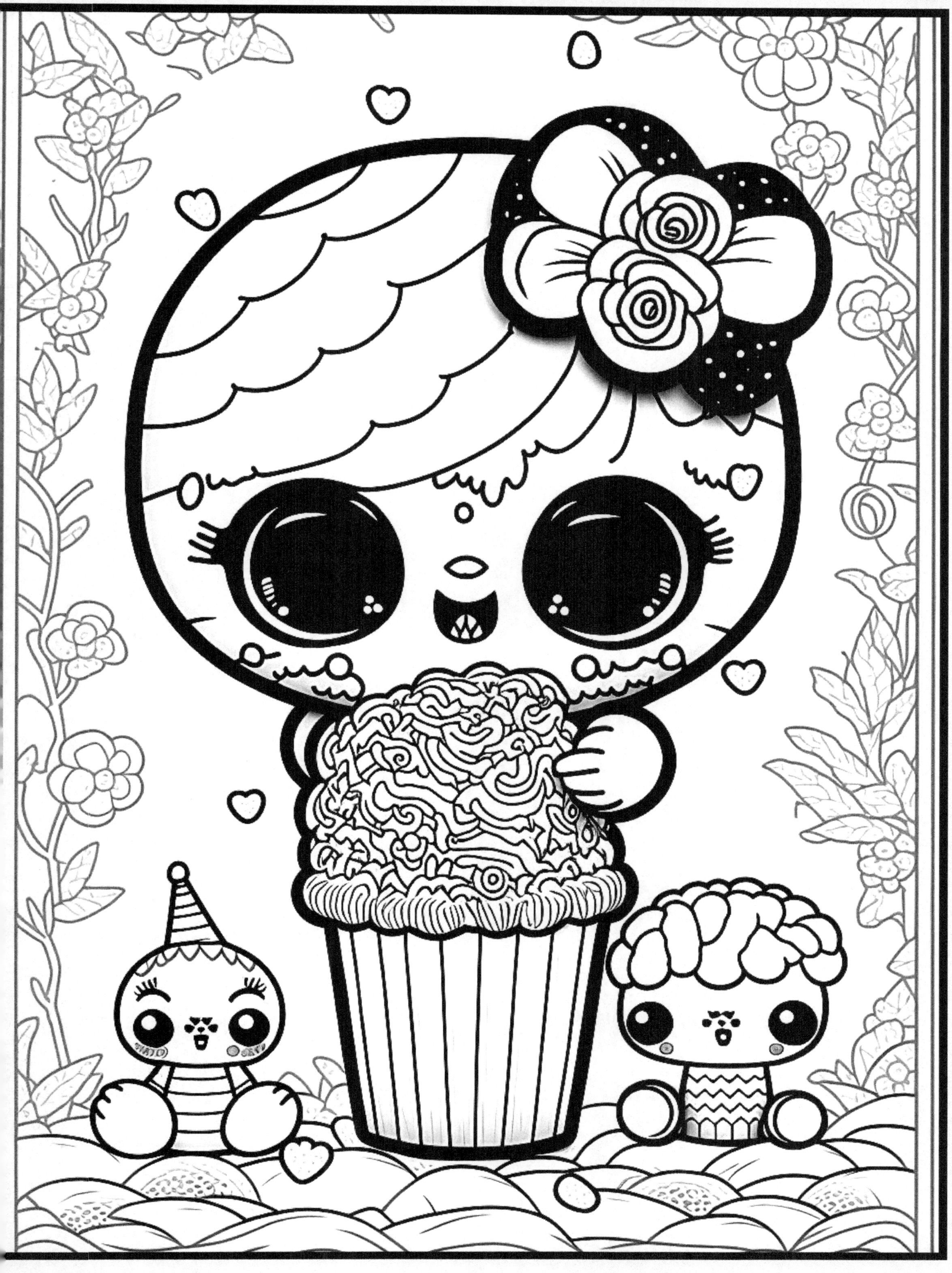

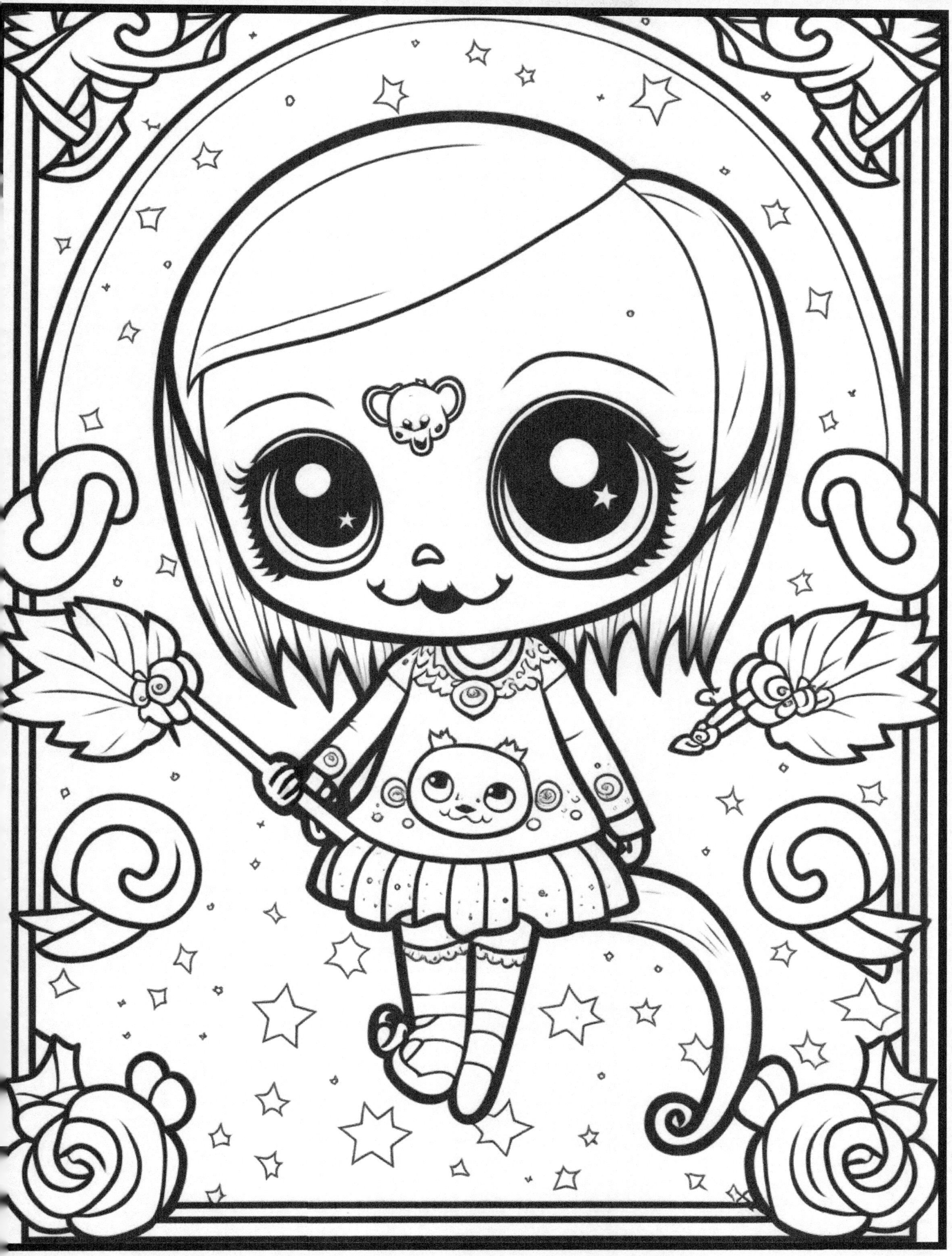

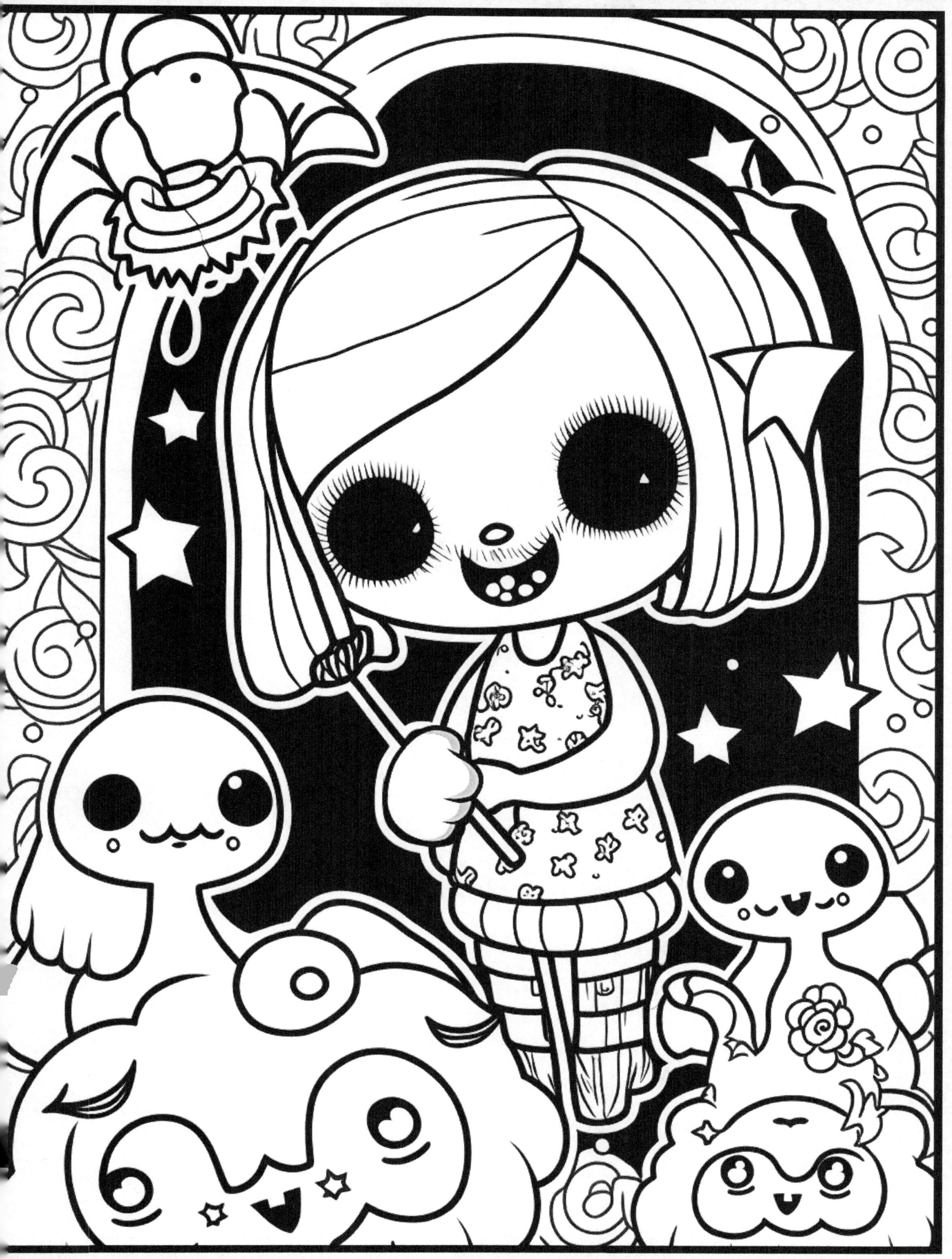

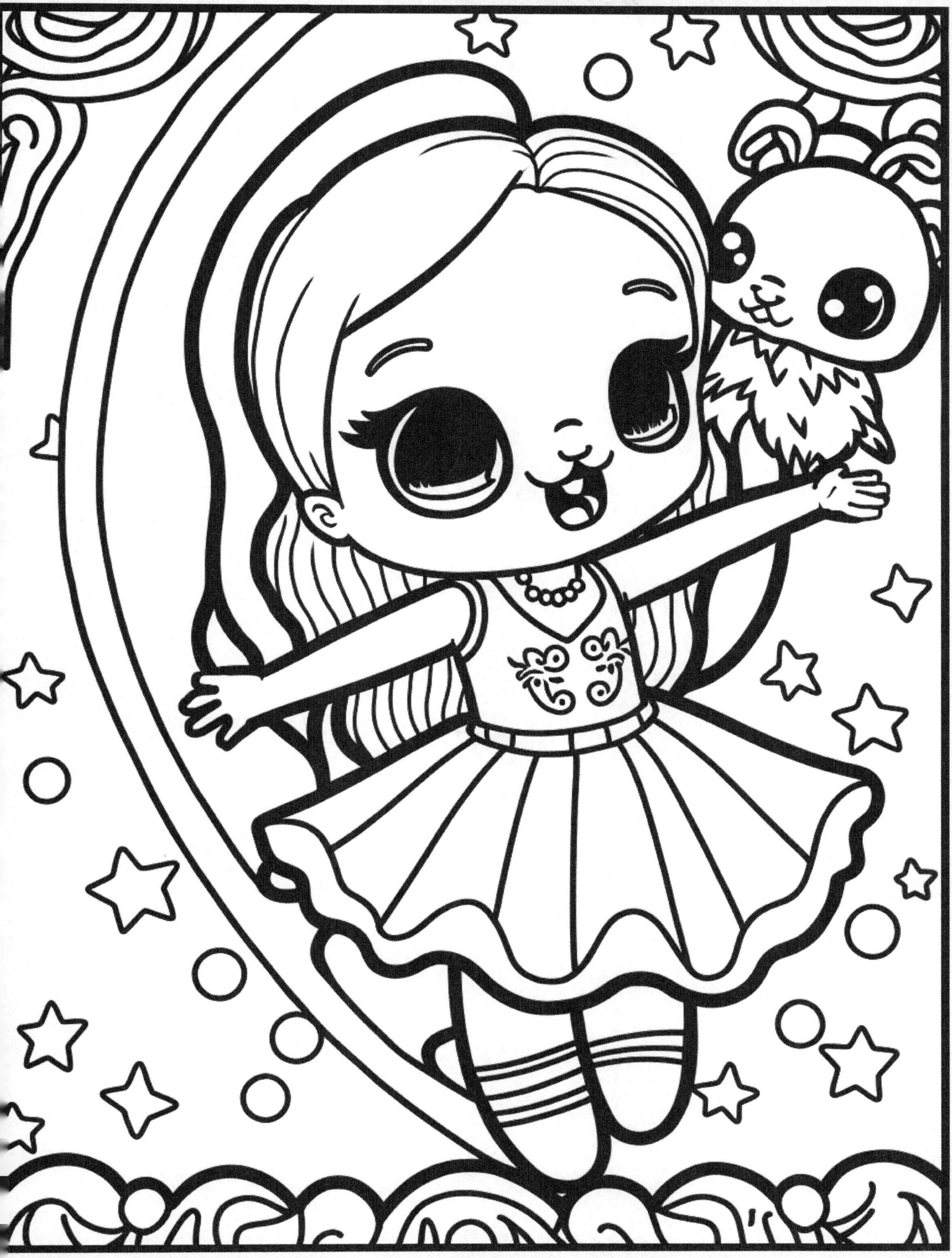

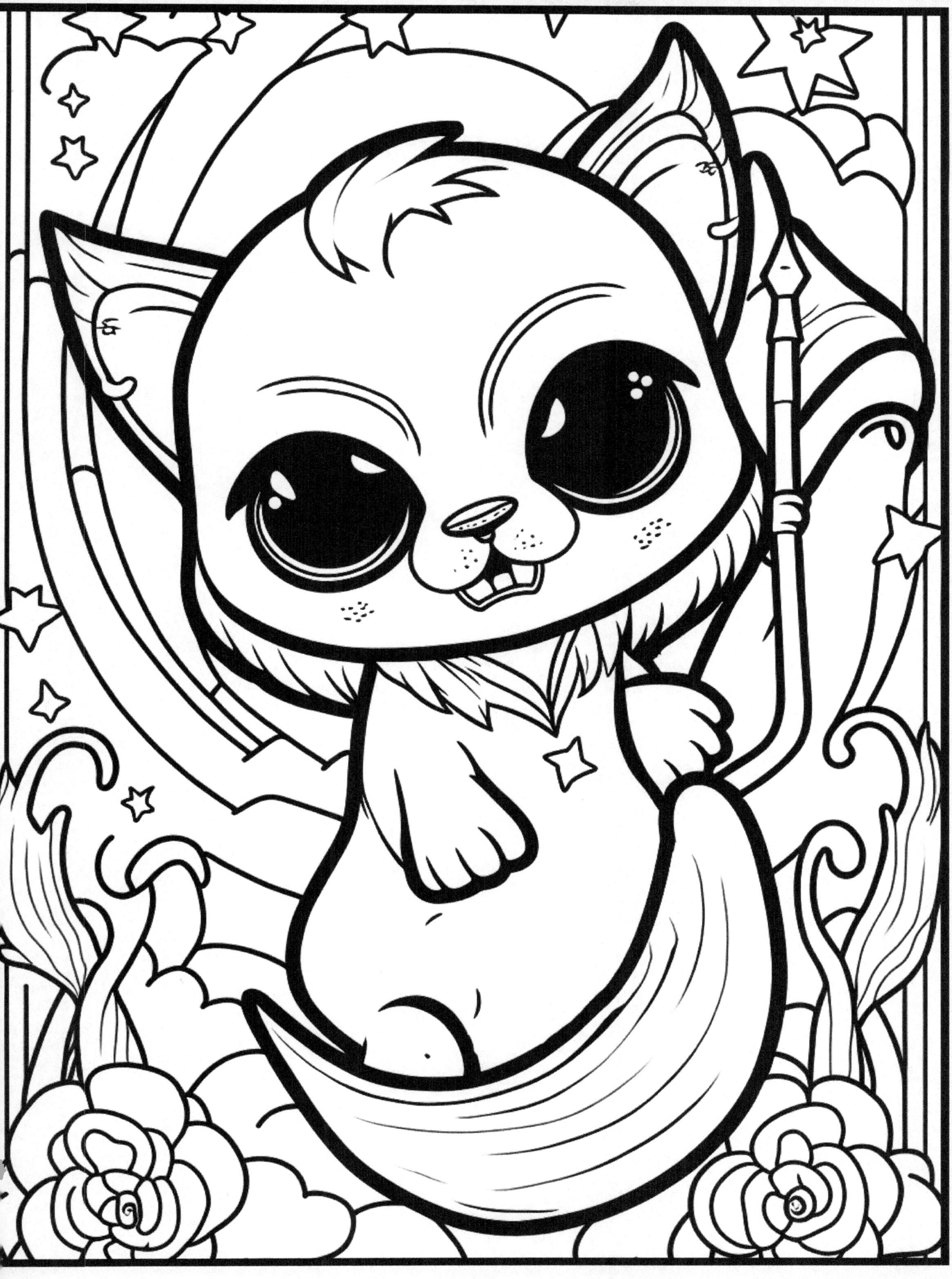

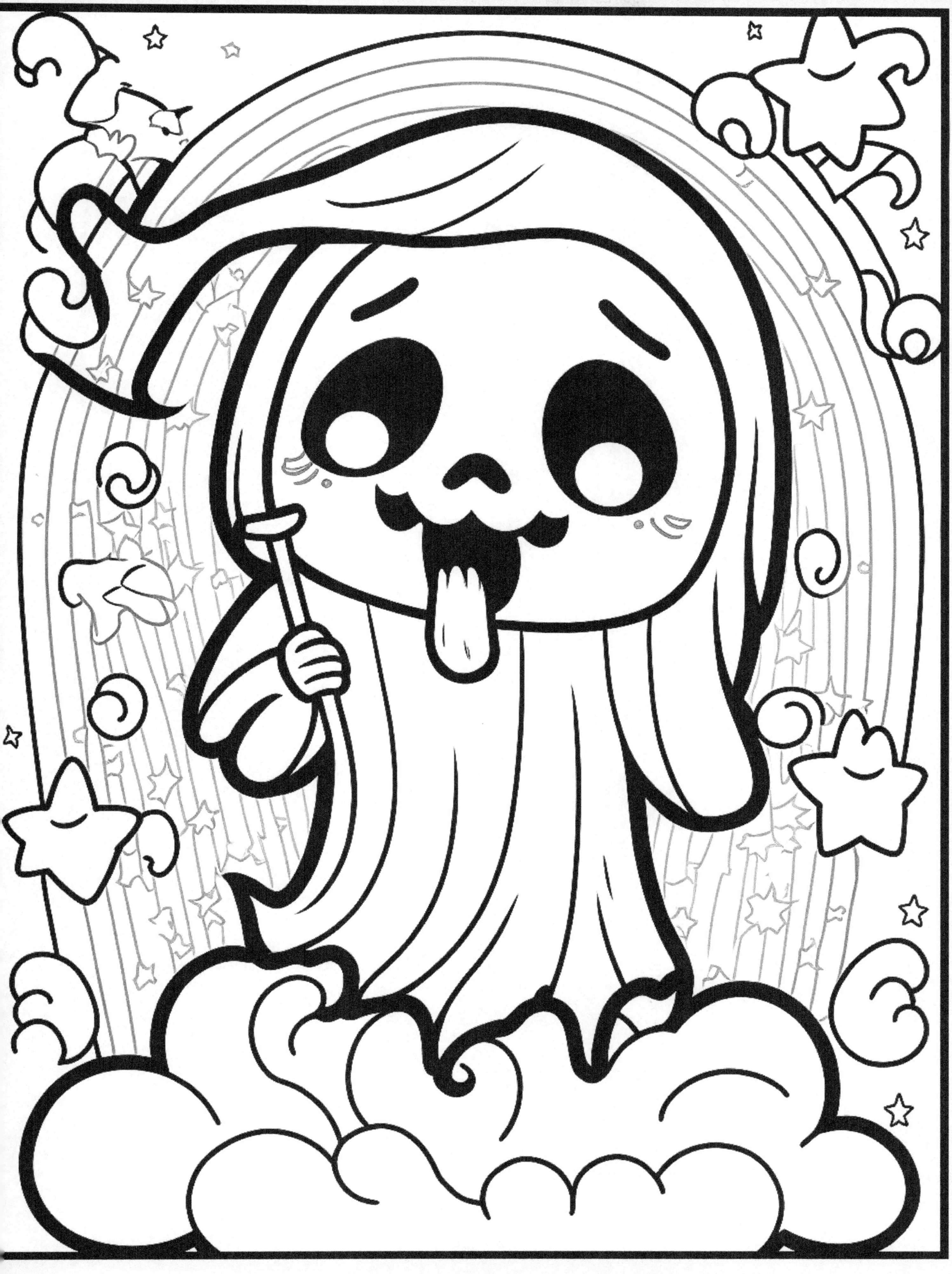

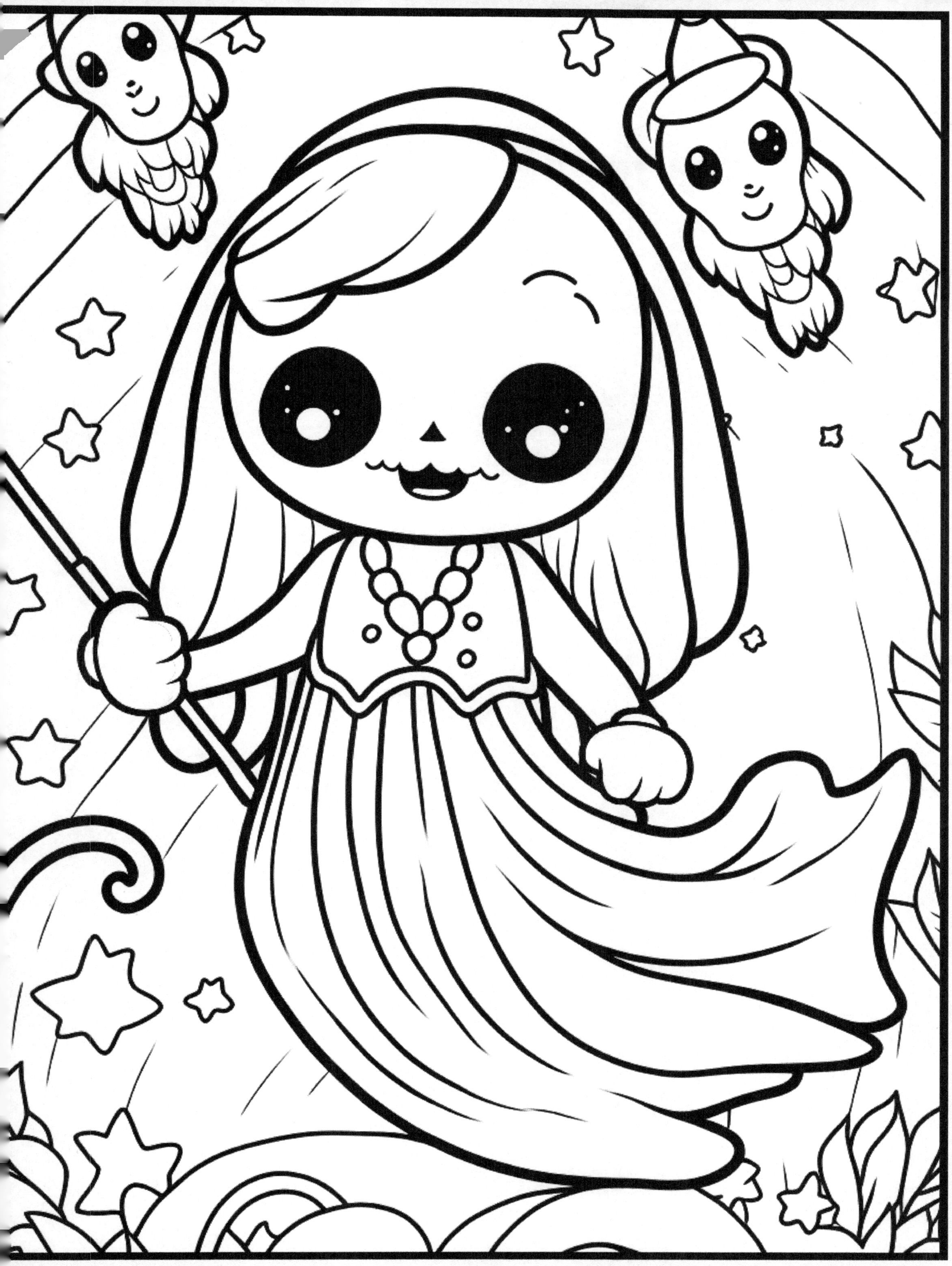

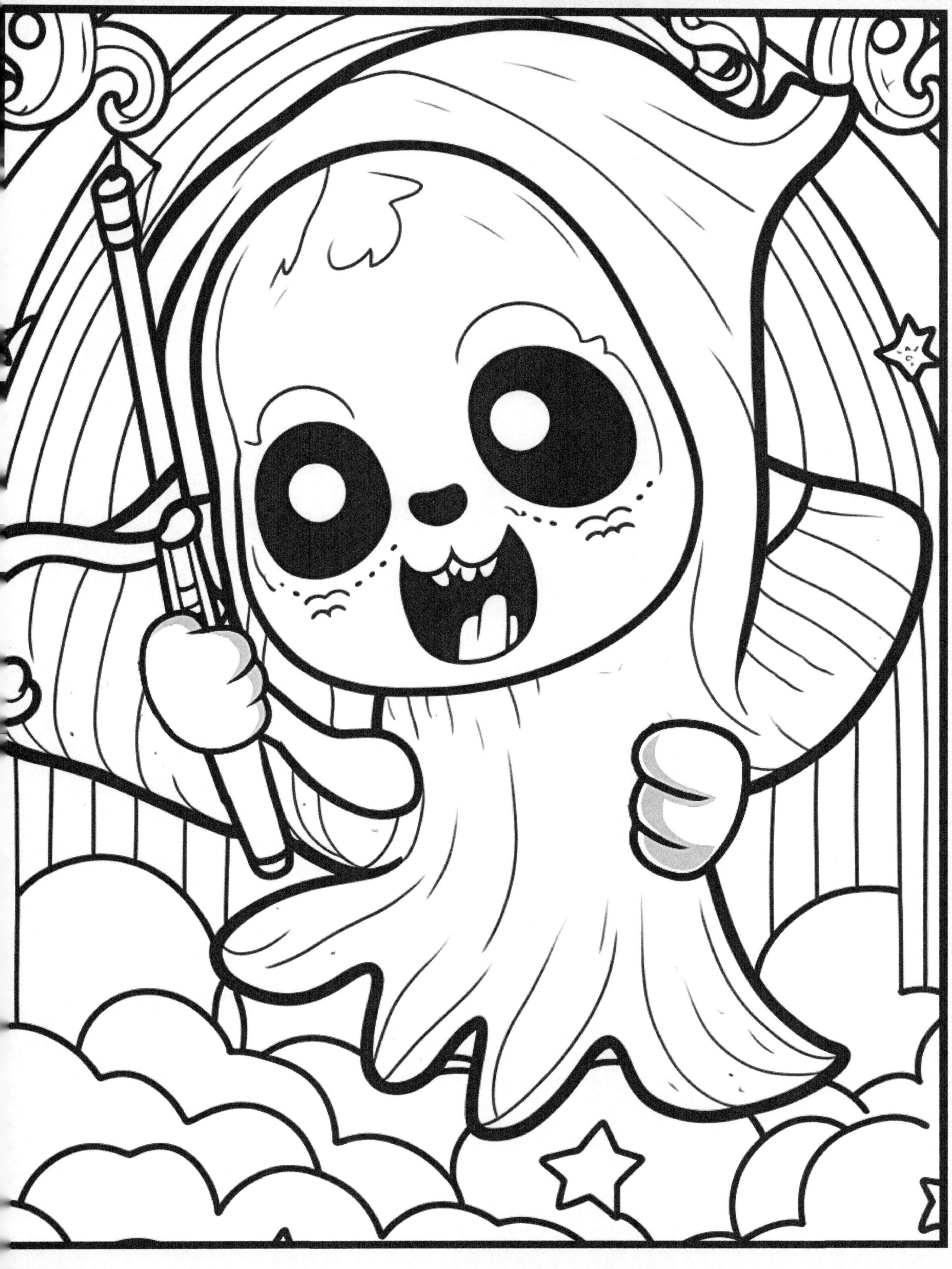

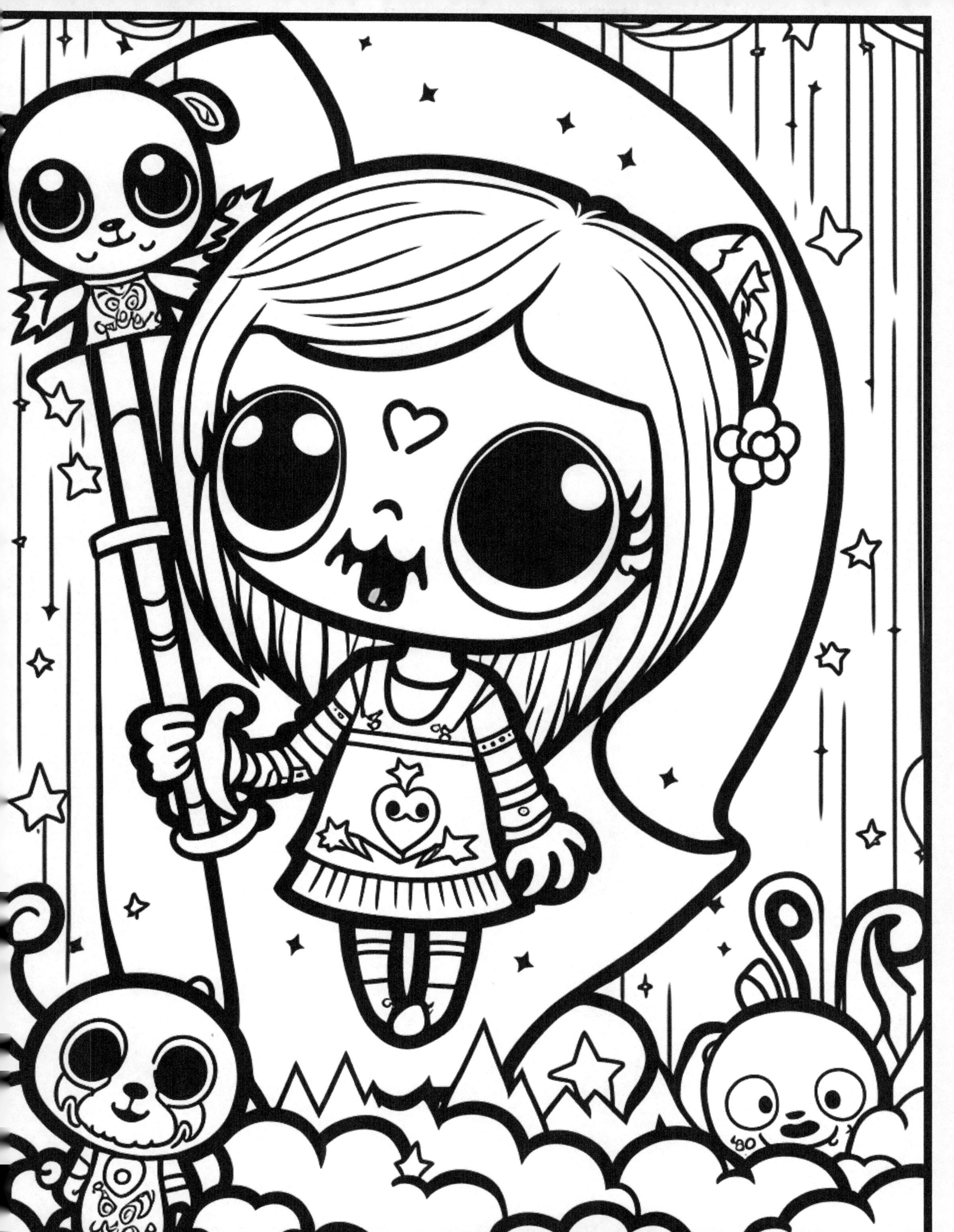

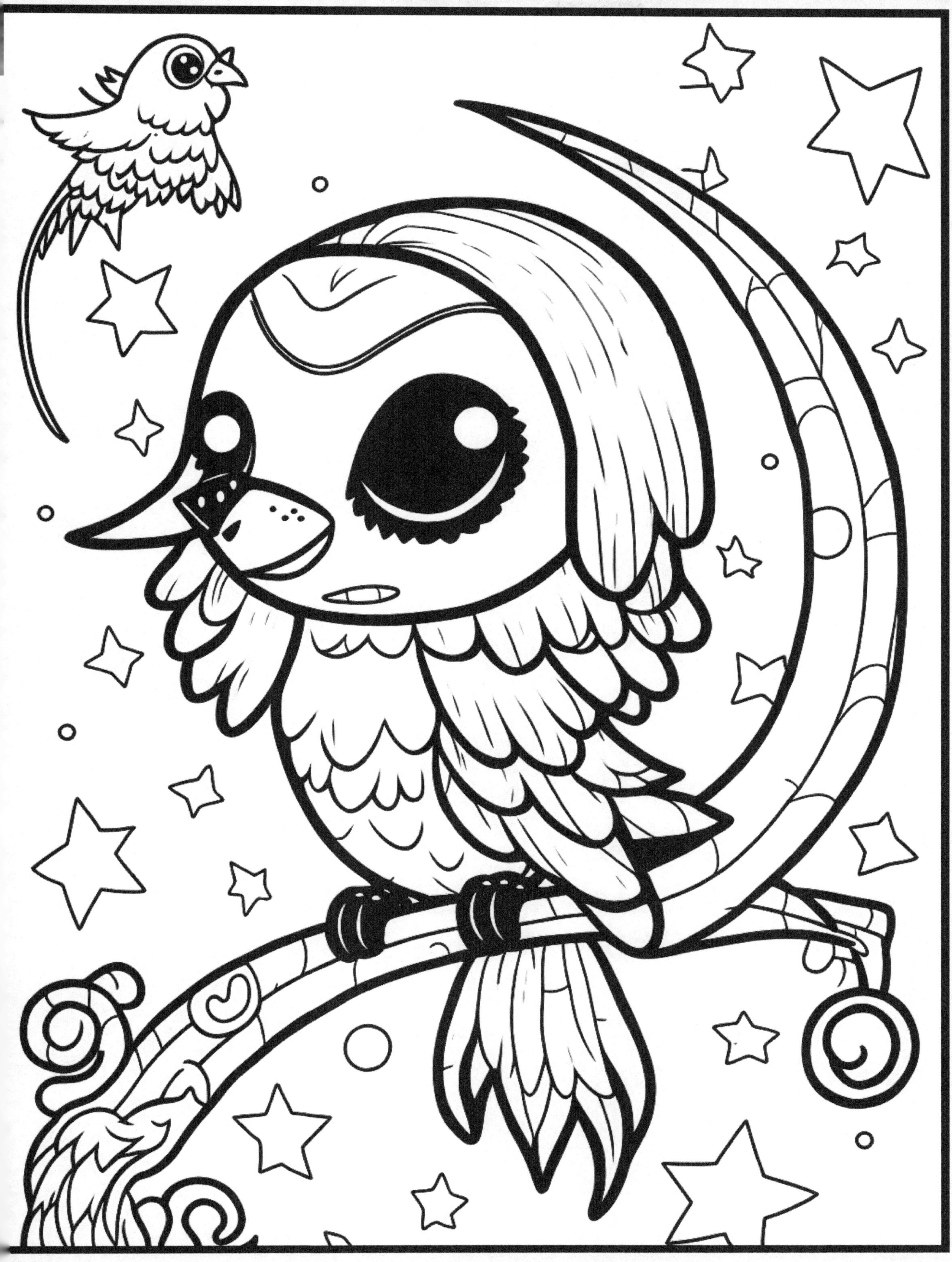

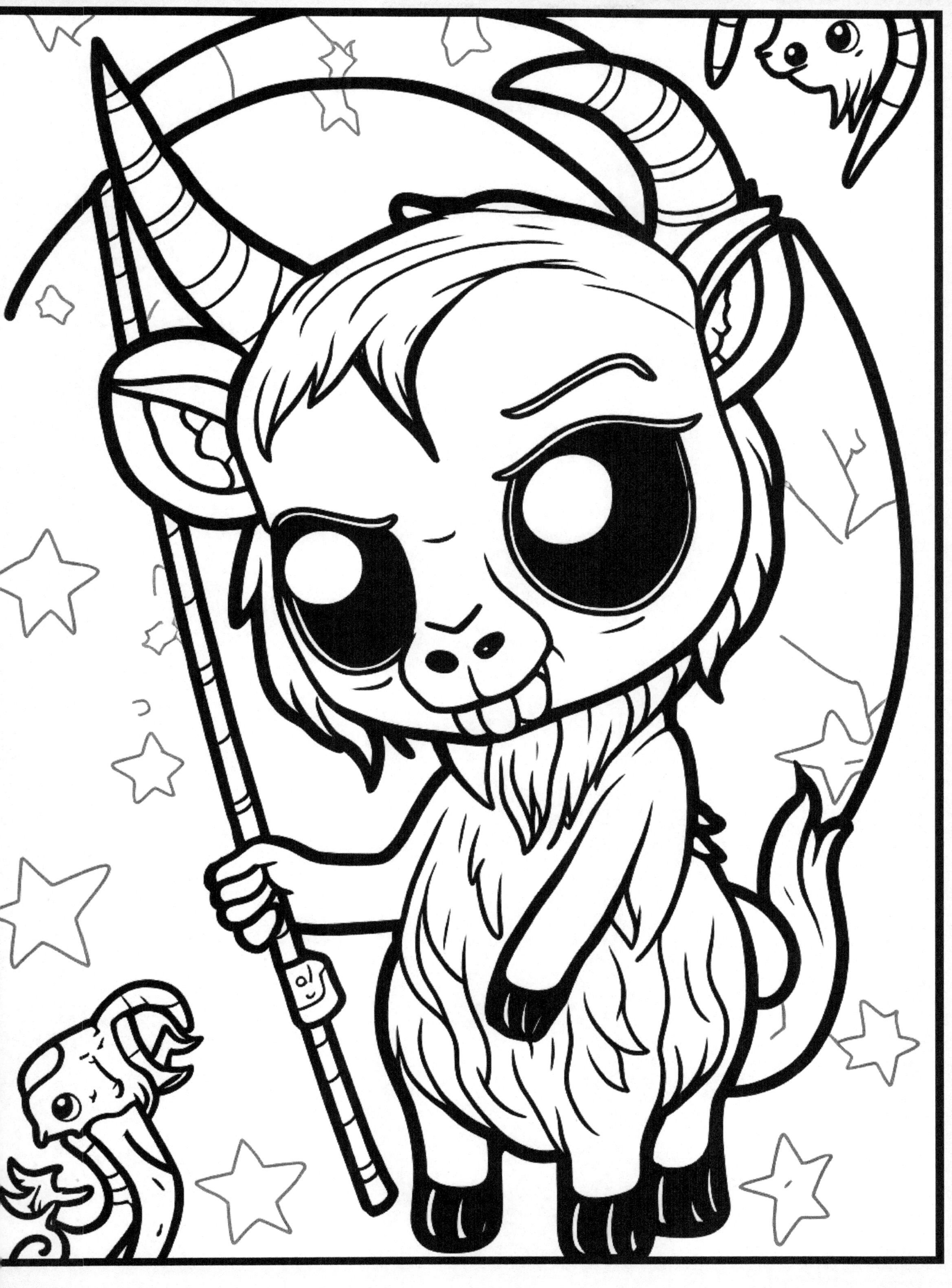

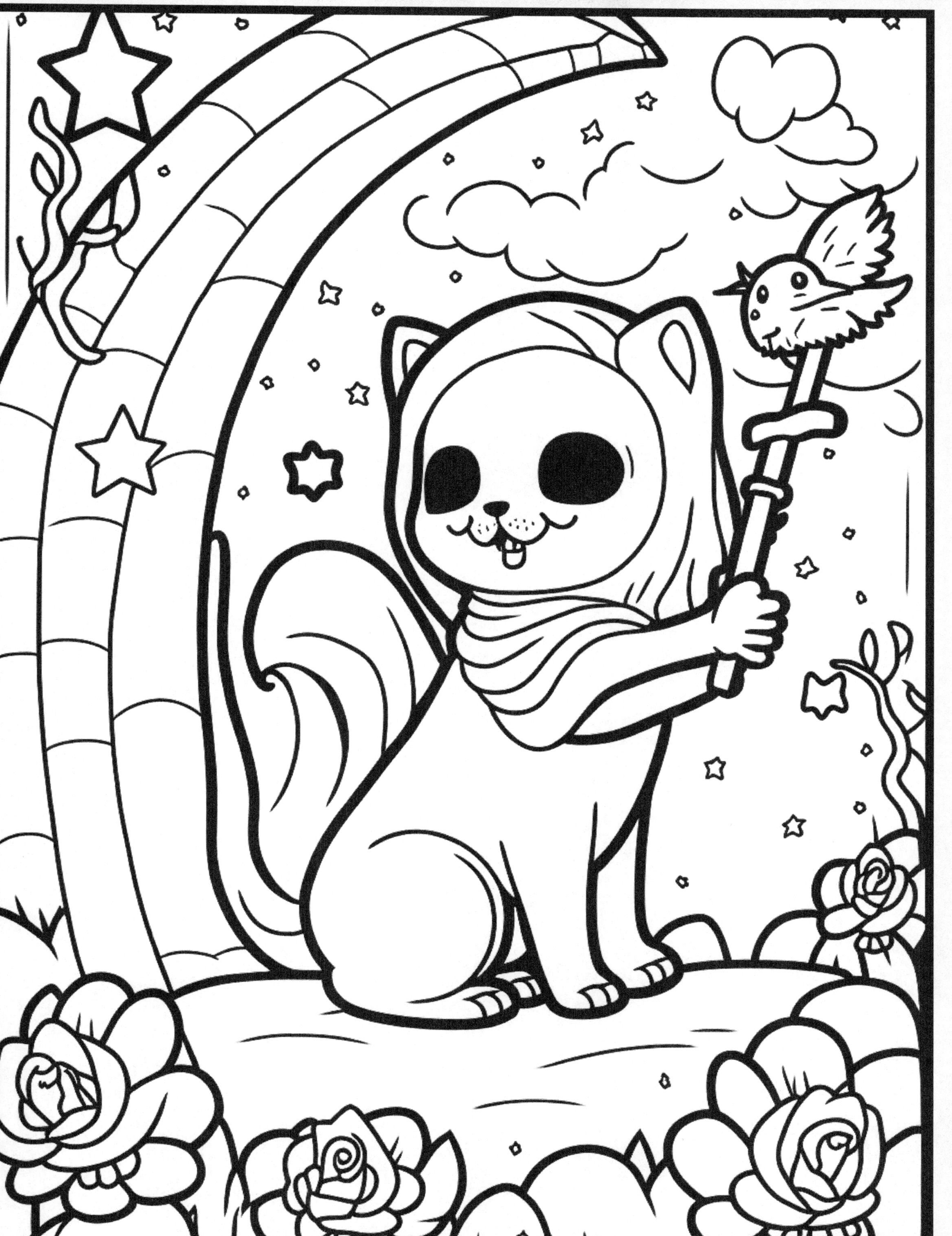

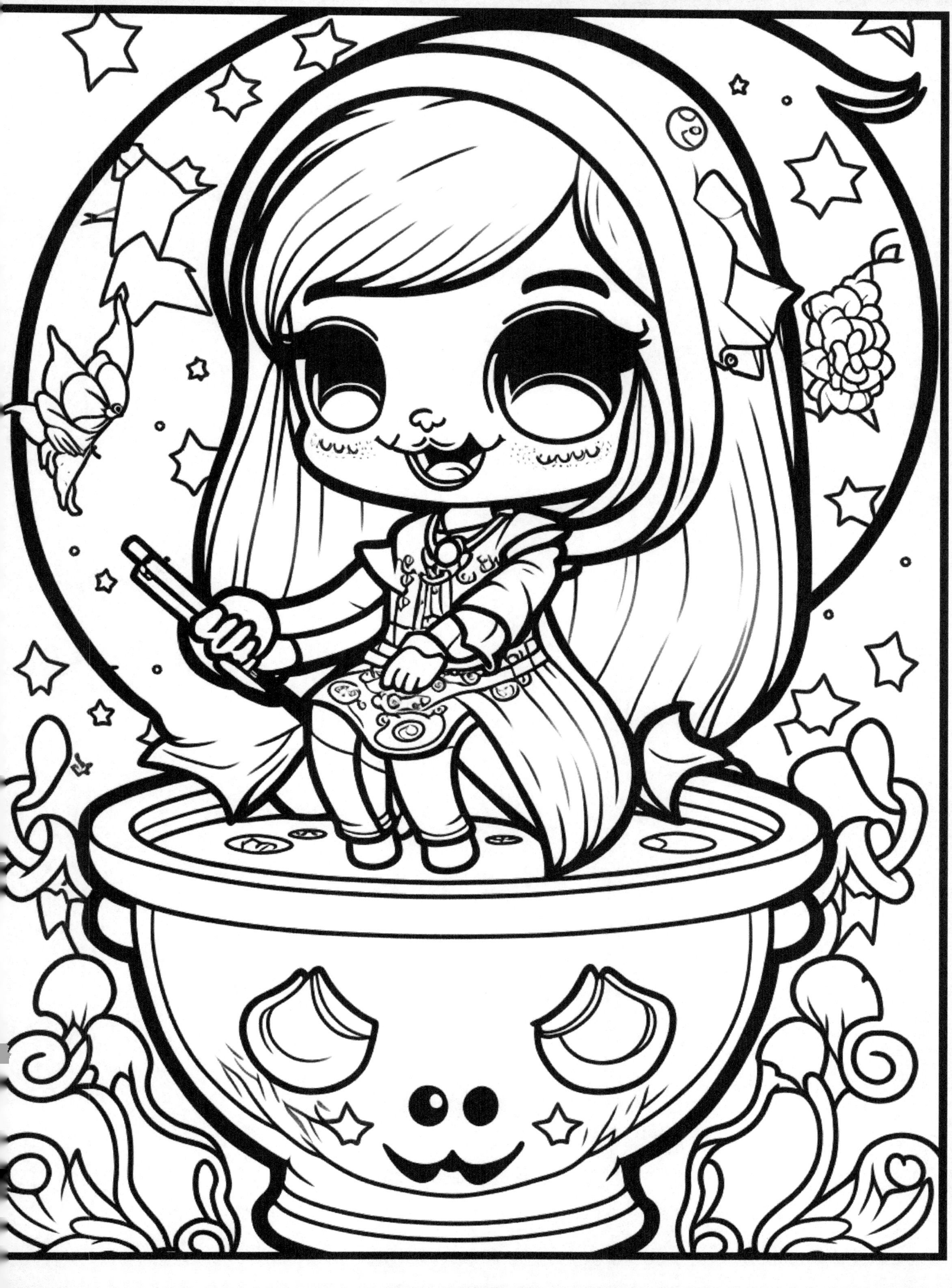

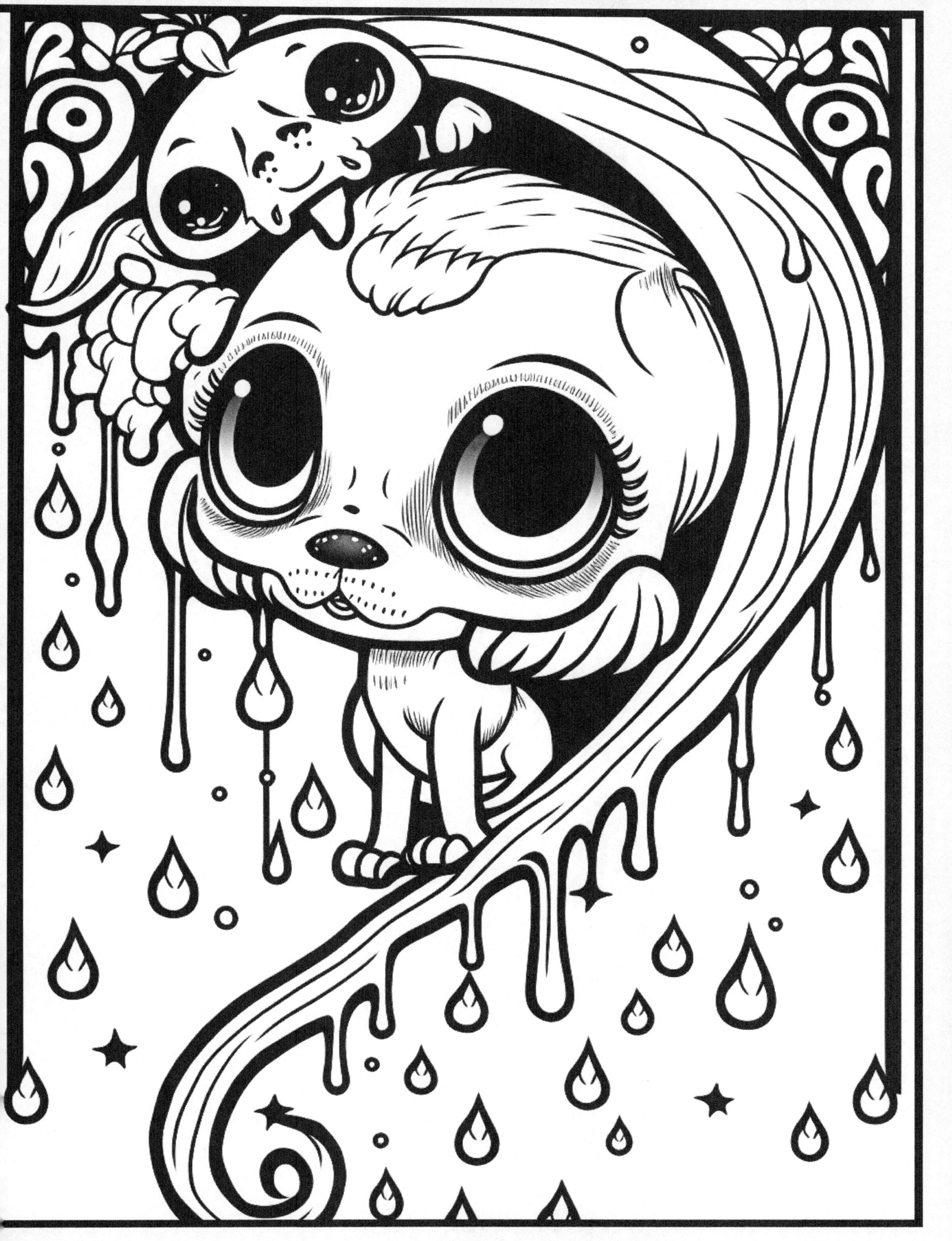

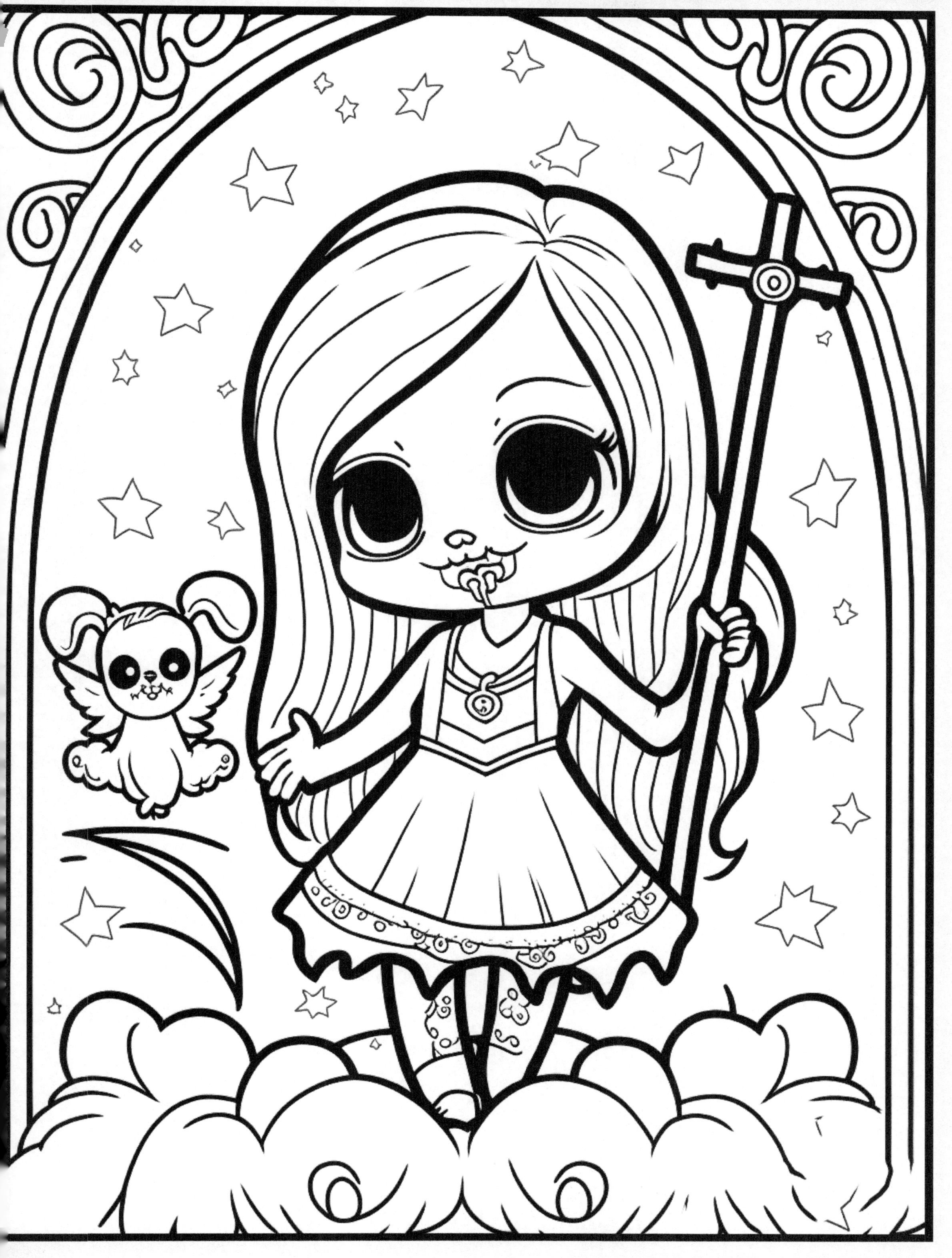

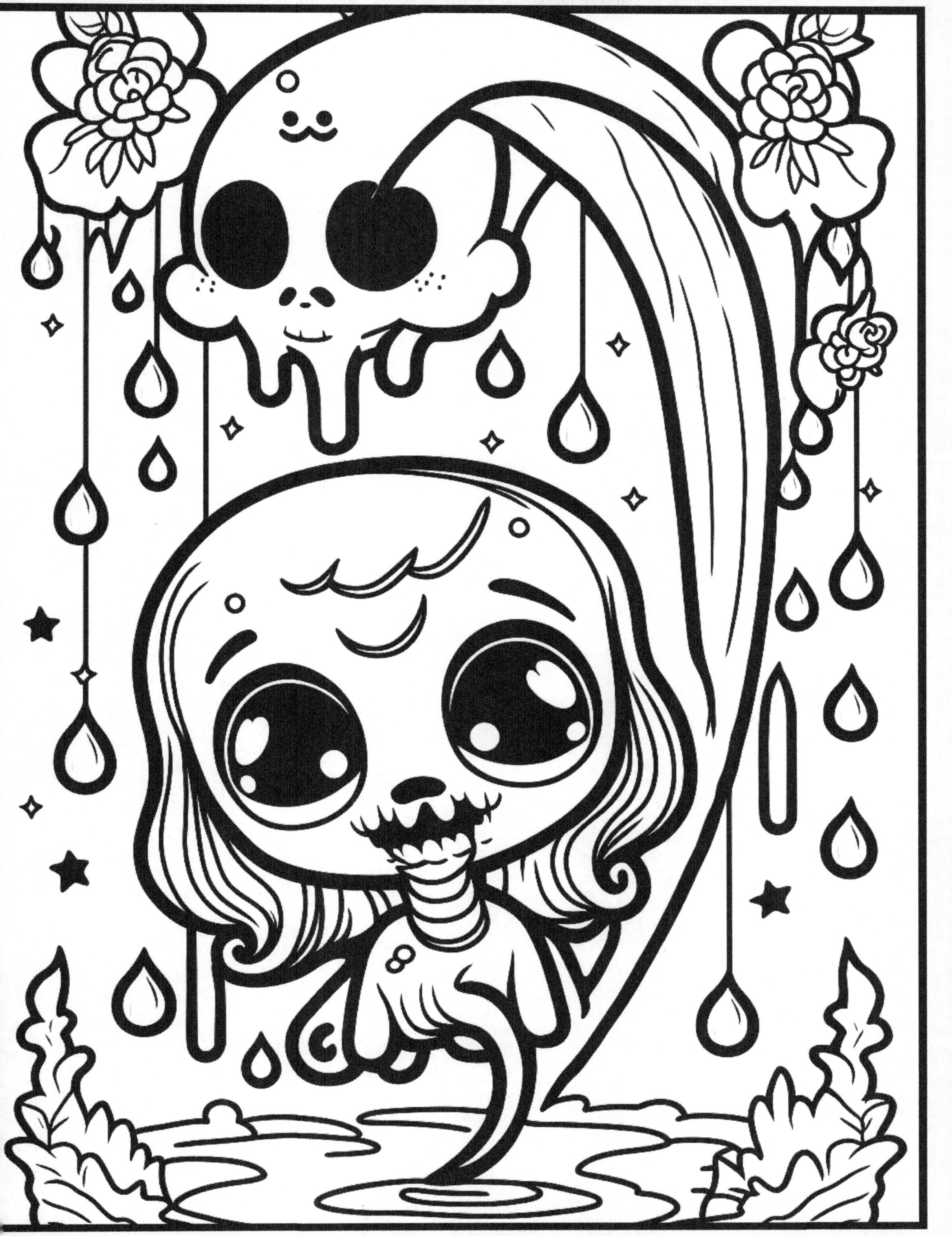

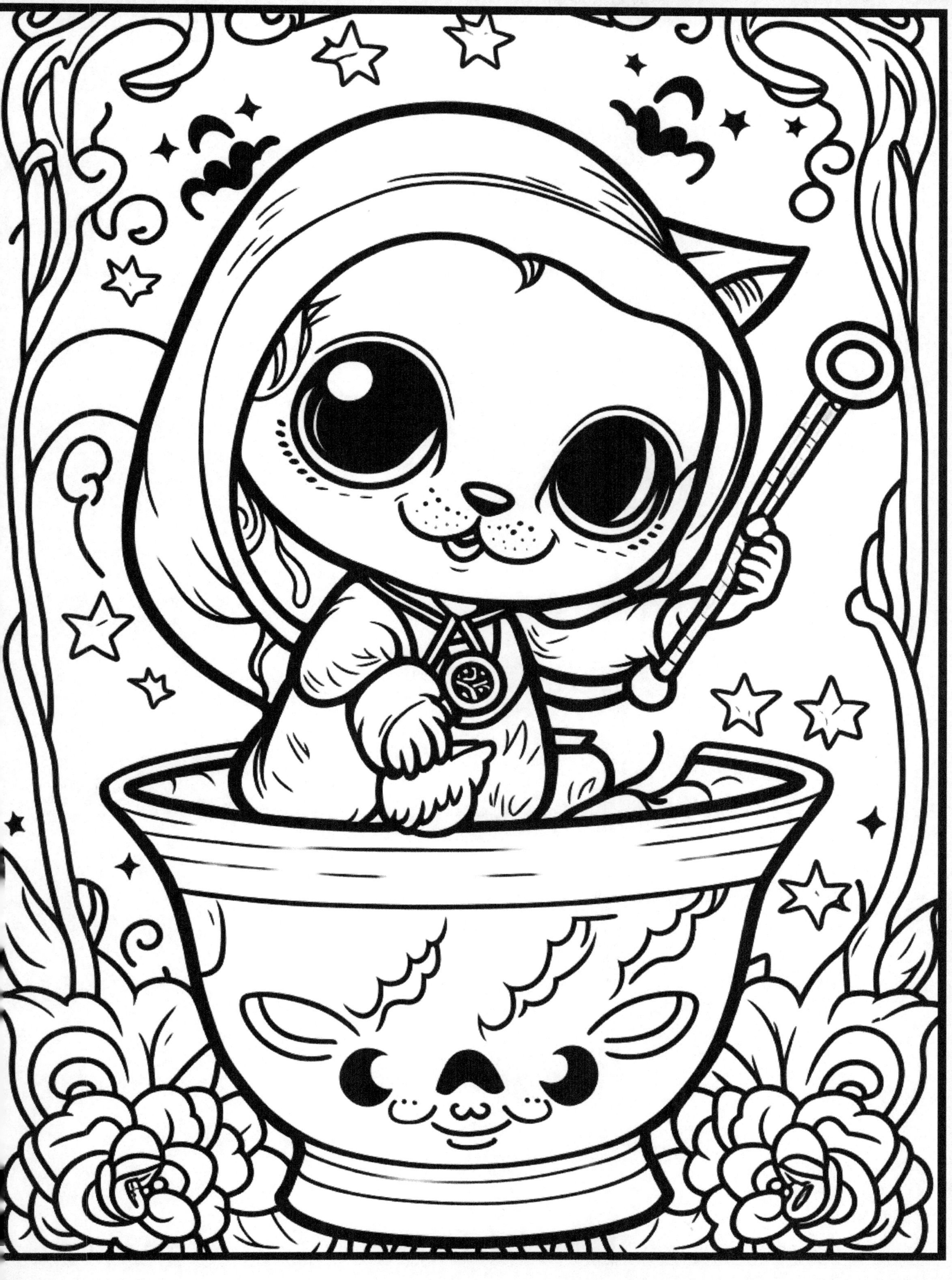

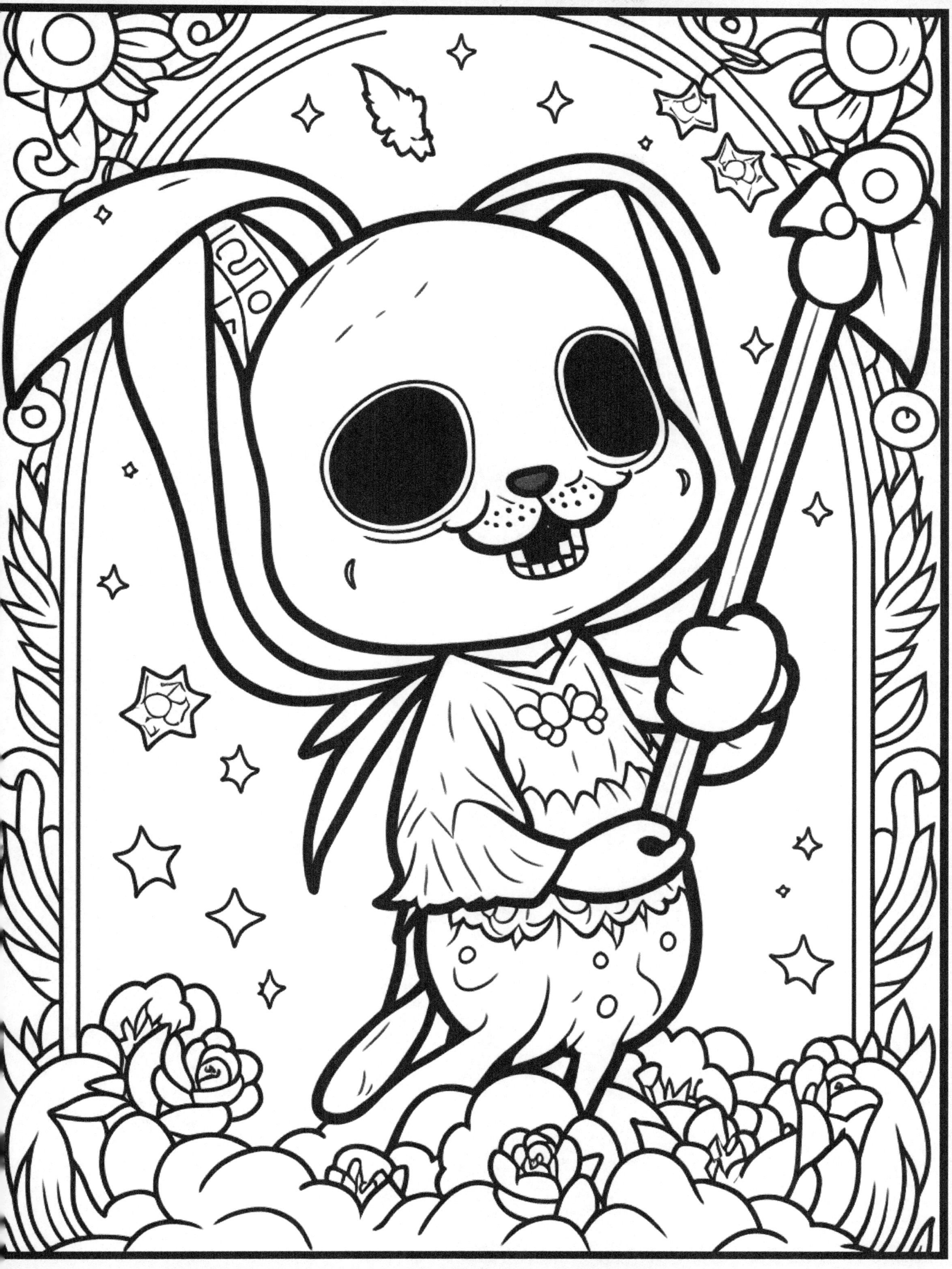

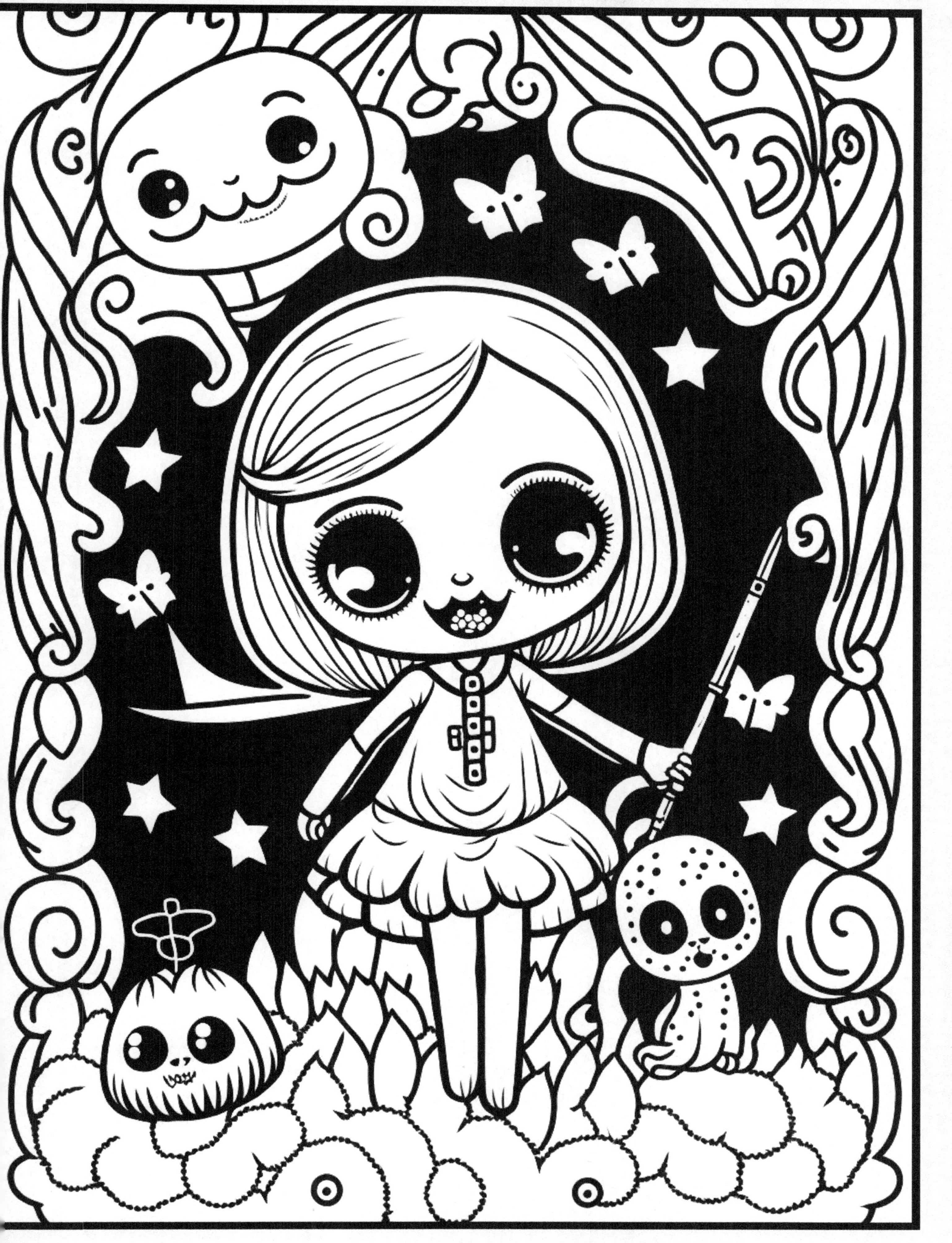

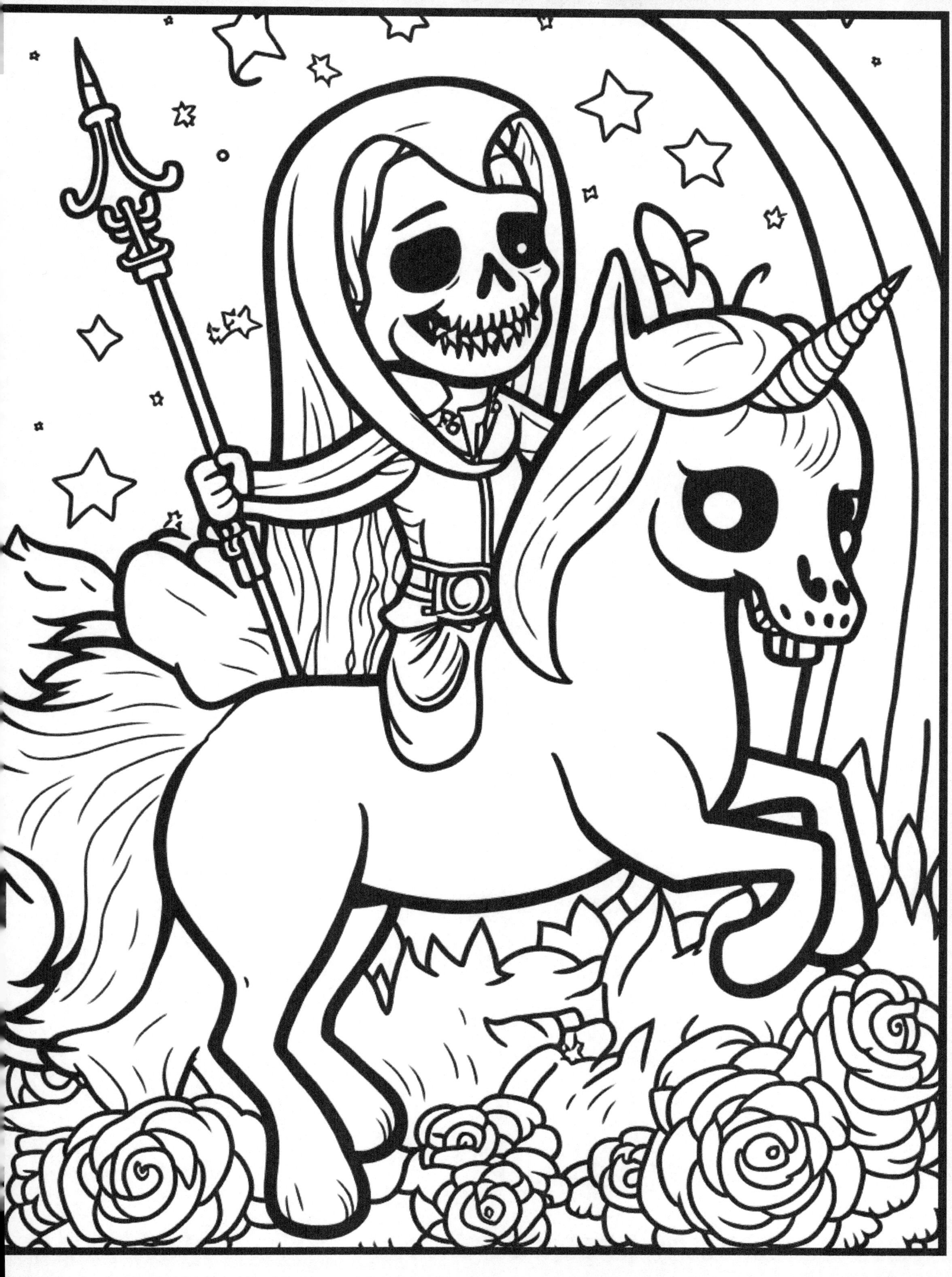

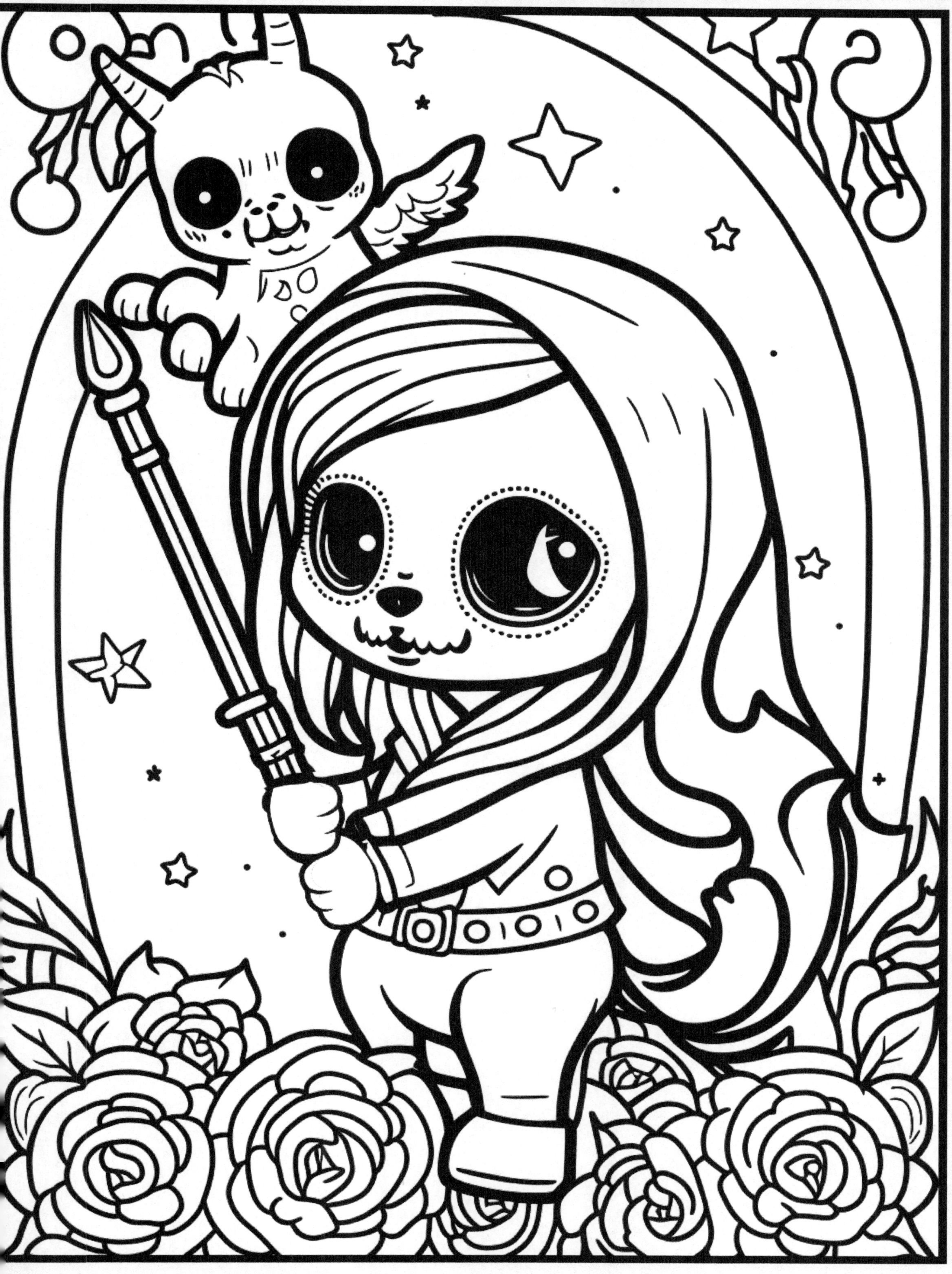

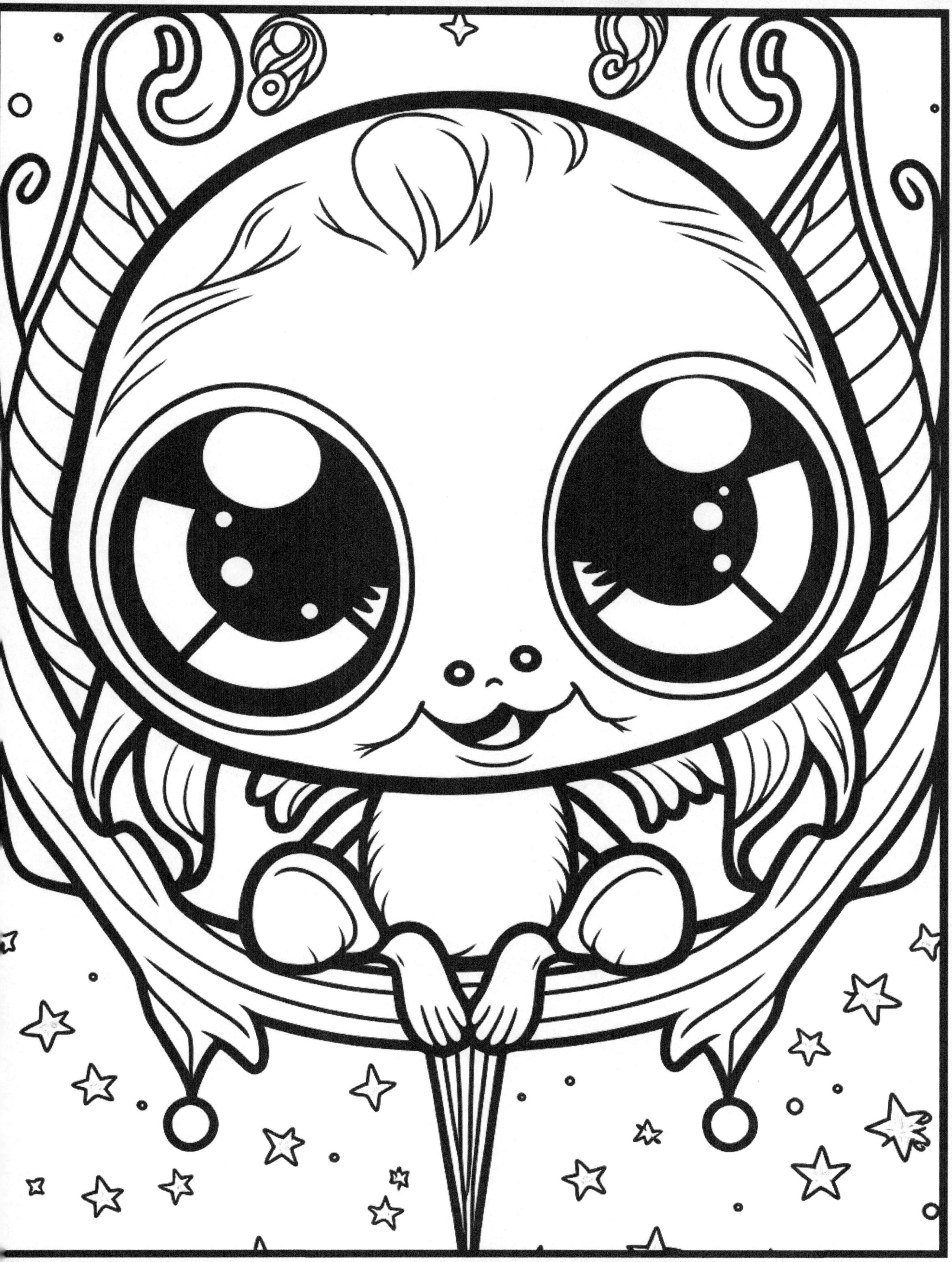

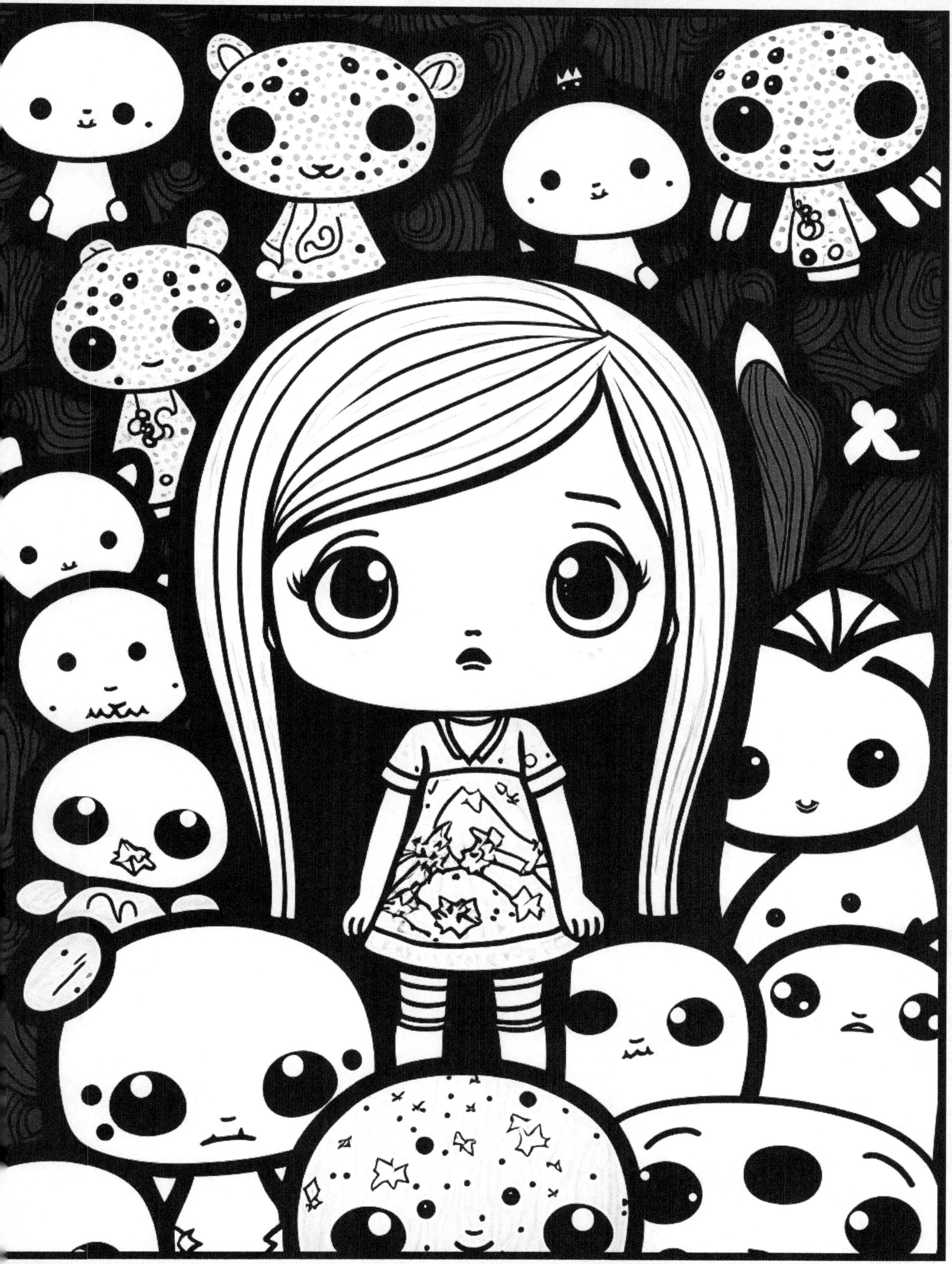

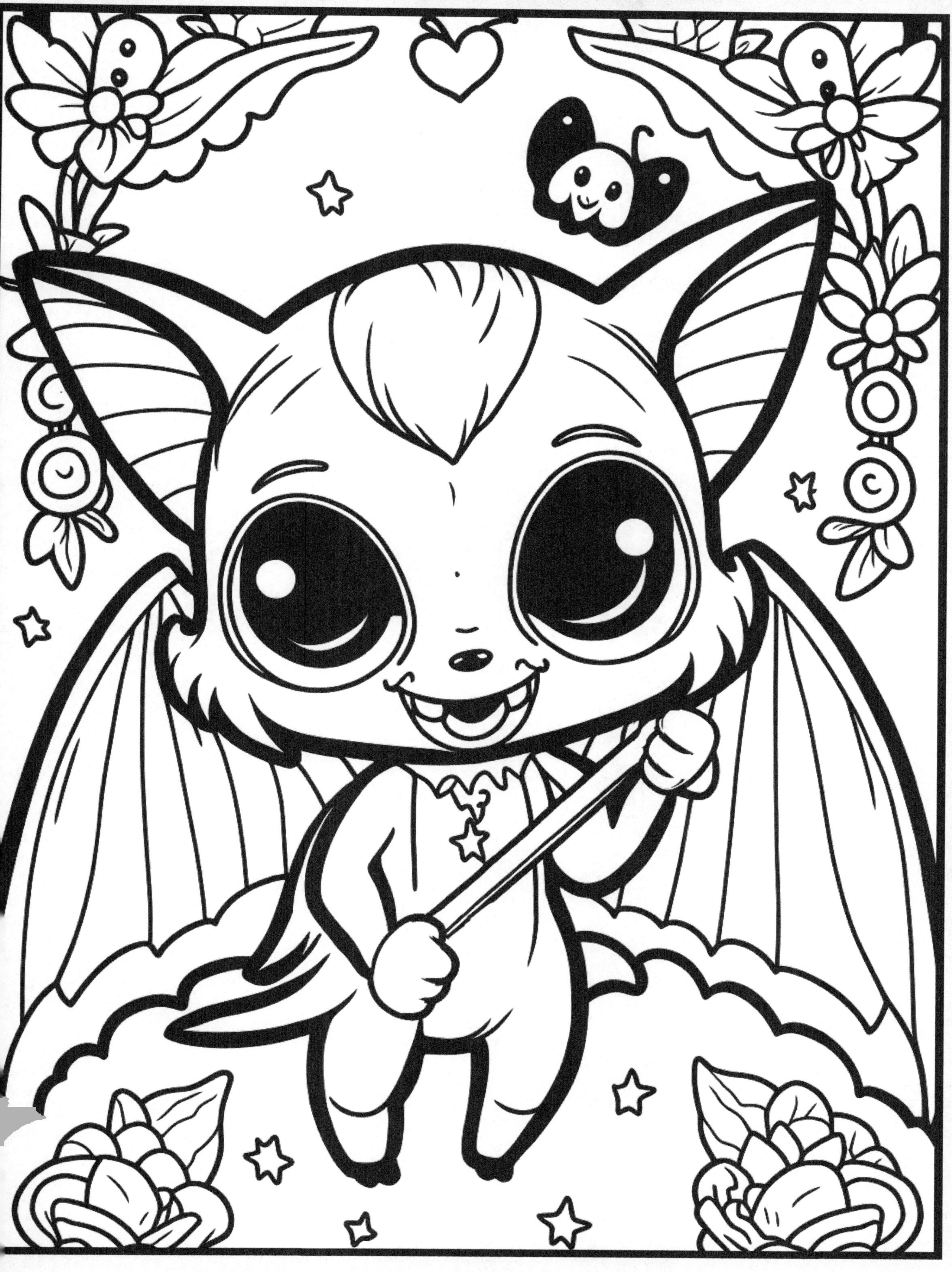

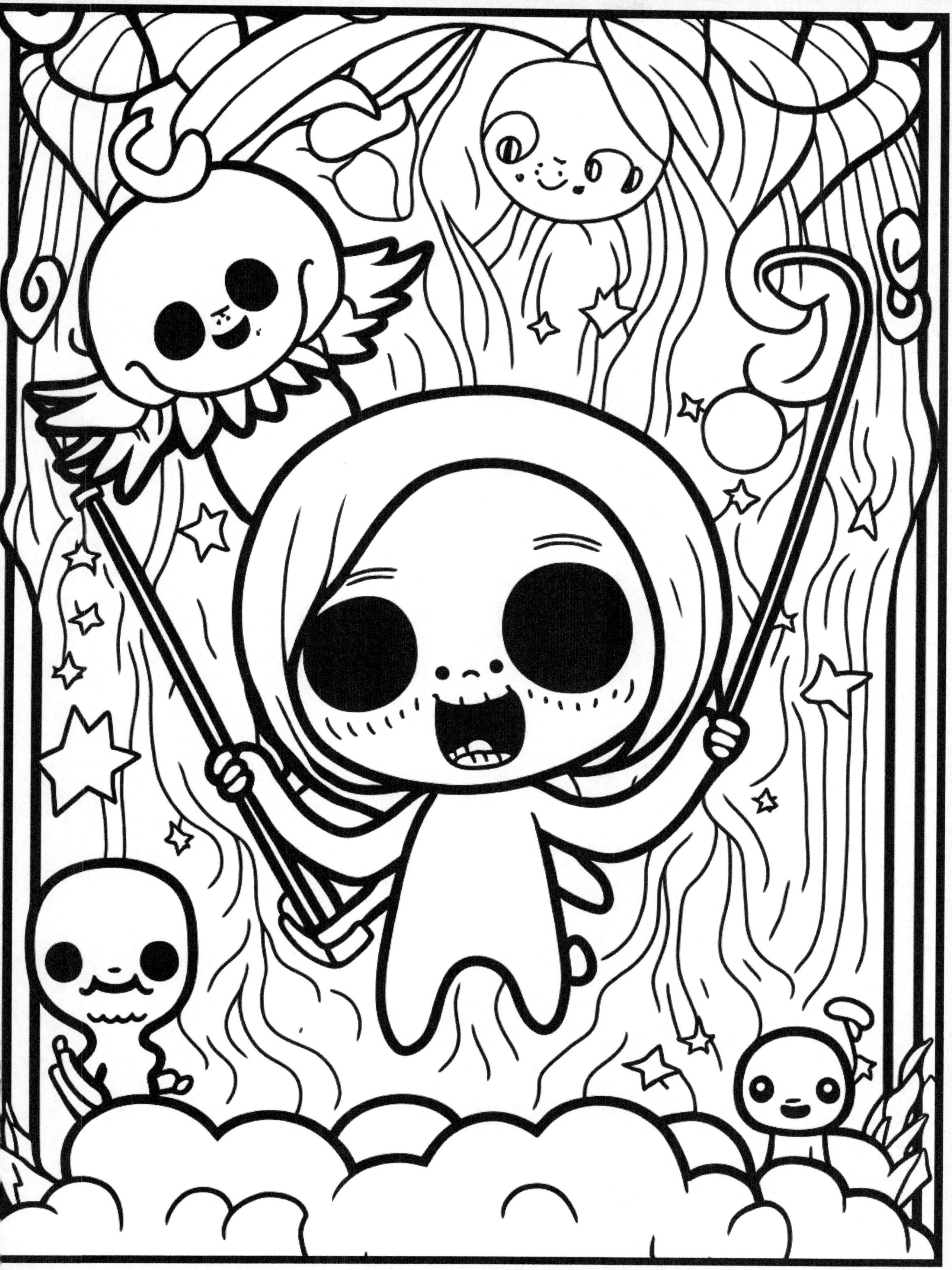

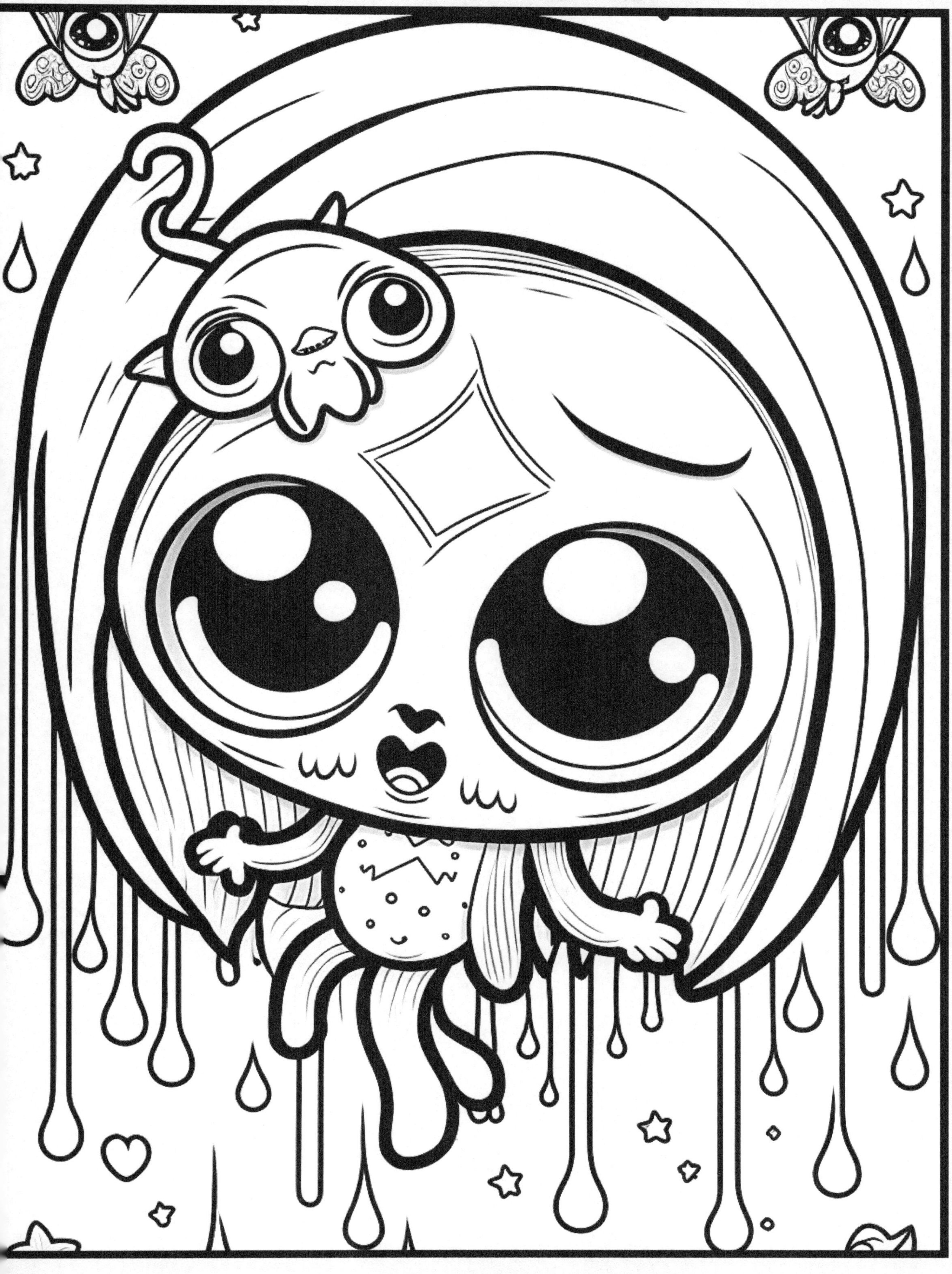

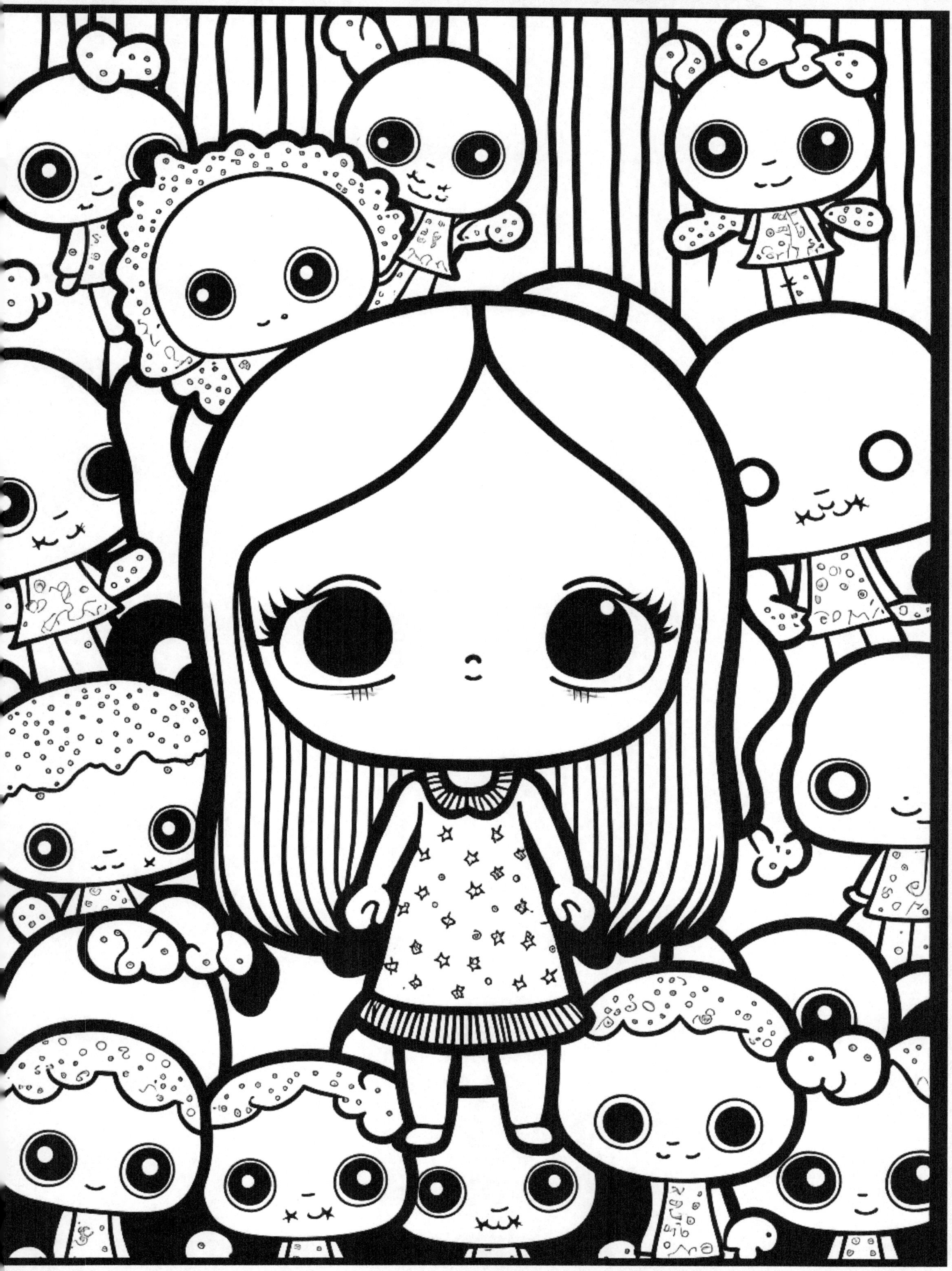

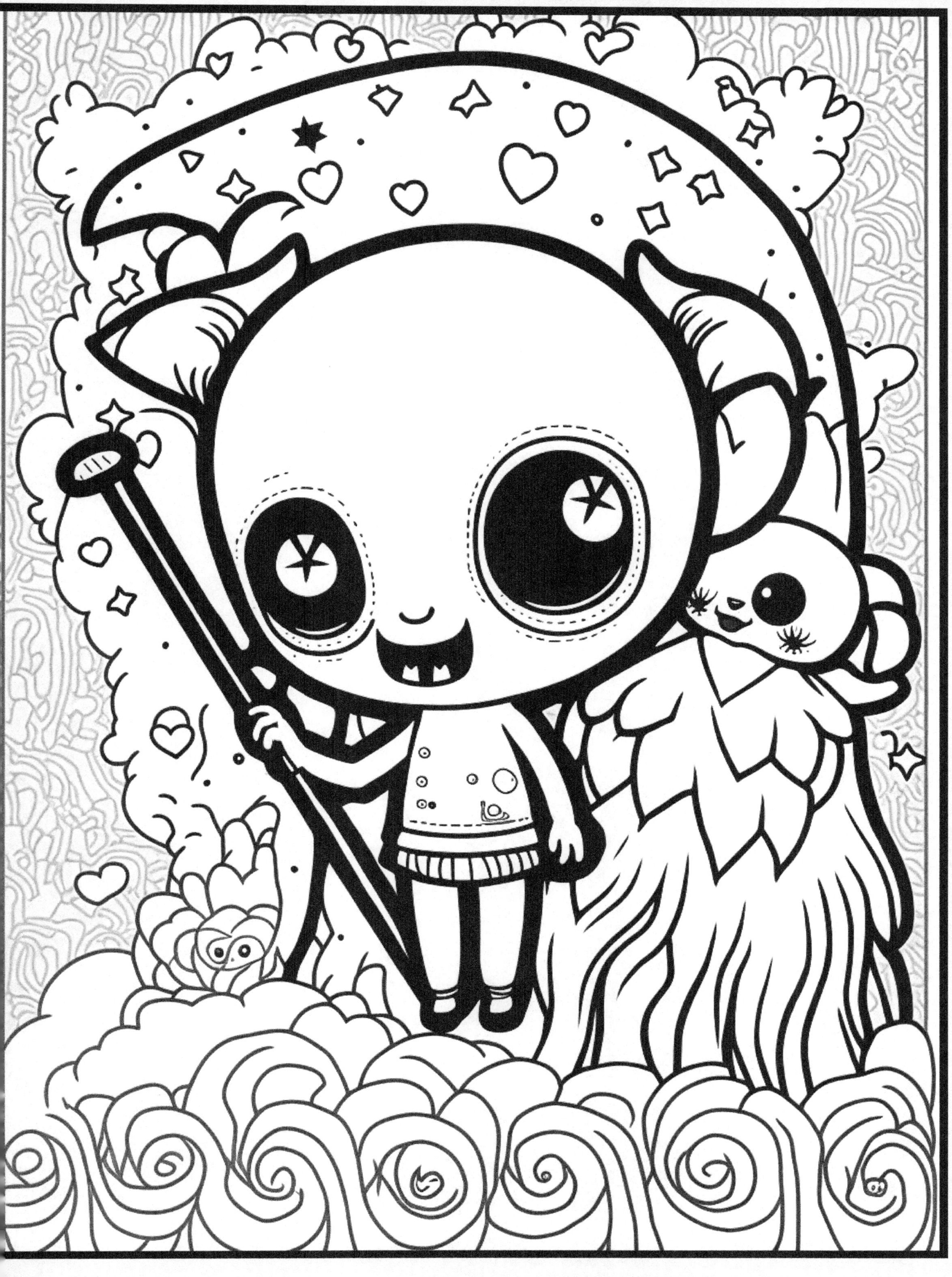

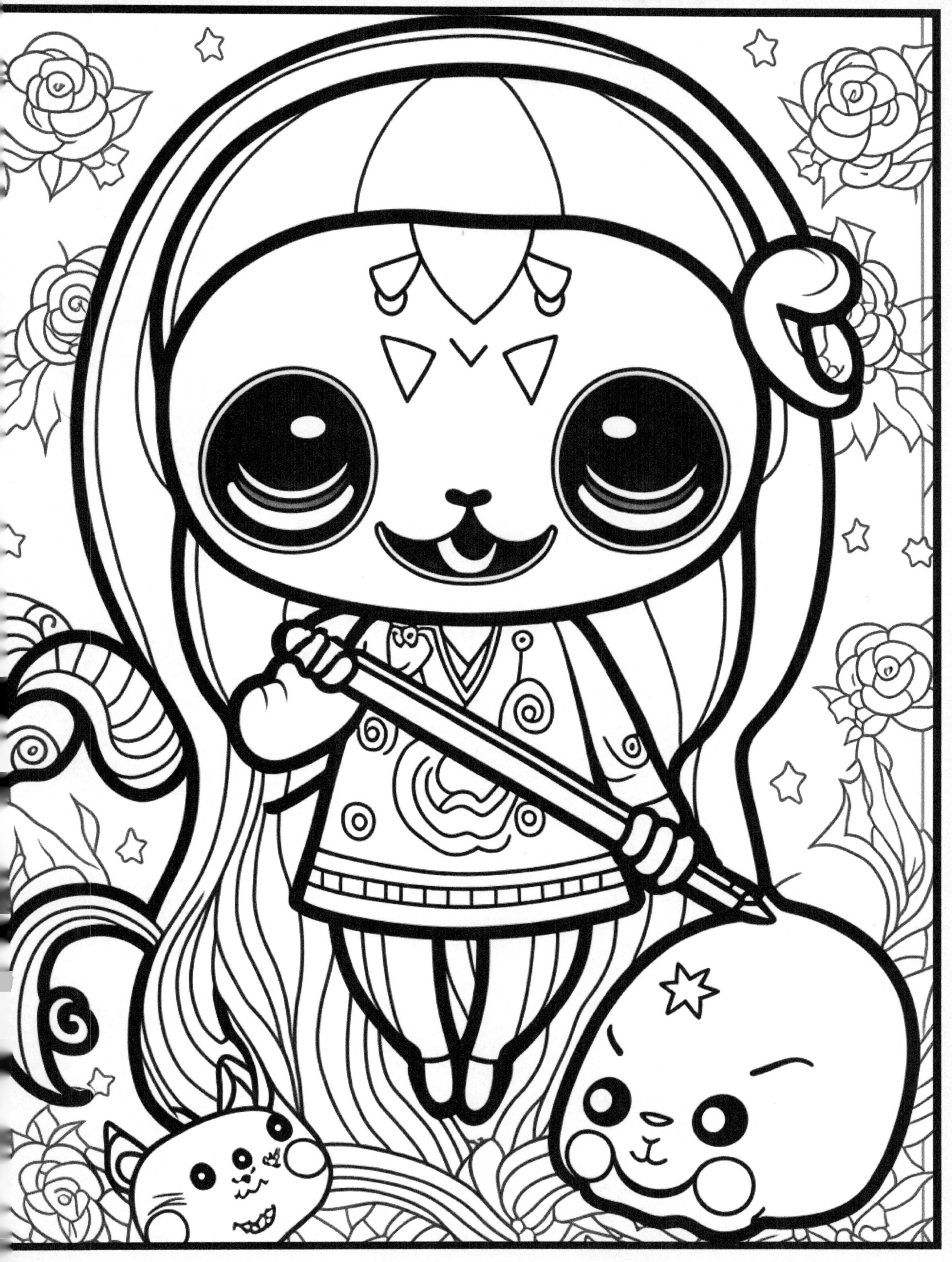

Thank you so much for choosing our coloring book!
We hope you enjoyed it and had a wonderful experience. If you have a moment, would you kindly consider leaving us a review? As a small business, your feedback means the world to us and helps us grow. It only takes a few seconds, and we genuinely appreciate your support.